Living a Life Pleasing to God

You Can Do It – With His Help!

WALTER ALBRITTON

Other Books by the Author

He Took My Hand

Precious Memories of Dean Albritton

Living a Life Filled with Love

Jesus is Everything

GLORY!

Be Strong and Courageous

Struggling with Grief, Finding Peace

Changing Your World

Living in Christ – the Only Way to Live

Life's Greatest Adventure – Serving Jesus Christ

Measure Your Life By Breathtaking Moments

When You Lose Someone You Love

God is Not Done with You

When Your Heart is Broken

The Great Secret

233 Days

If You Want to Walk on Water, You've Got to Get Out of Your Boat

Leaning On the Banisters of Heaven

Life is Short So Laugh Often, Live Fully and Love Deeply

Just Get Over It and Move On!

Don't Let Go of the Rope!

The Four Gospels (Commentary on Selected Passages)

Paul's Letters (Commentary on Selected Passages)

Beacons of Hope (Selected Passages of the New Testament)

Scripture quotations unless otherwise indicated are from The Holy Bible, New International Version, NIV, used by permission of Zondervan.

Printed in the United States of America
By Bingham Bend Publishers

Book design 2025 by Susan Heslup

Ordering information:
This book may be purchased in paperback or kindle from Amazon.com or in paperback from walteralbritton7@gmail.com

LIVING A LIFE PLEASING TO GOD/WALTER ALBRITTON

ISBN: 979-8-270038-01-4

Dedicated to

MATT O'REILLY

Whom I have loved since he was a Cub Scout seeking
my help to earn his God and Country Award,
now an influential leader in the resurging Methodist
movement to recapture John Wesley's doctrine
of entire sanctification,
the devoted husband of Naomi Jackson O'Reilly
and loving father of their three young disciples:
Patrick, Vivian and Jackson,
the strong and gentle shepherd of
Christ Church Birmingham in Alabama,
a Global Methodist Congregation,
author of *FREE TO BE HOLY, a Biblical Theology
of Sanctification*, that everyone needs to read,
and what means so much to me,
my confidant, dear friend, and my son in the faith.

Glory!!!

⁷ You learned about the Good News from Epaphras, our beloved co-worker. He is Christ's faithful servant, and he is helping us on your behalf. ⁸ He has told us about the love for others that the Holy Spirit has given you. ⁹ So we have not stopped praying for you since we first heard about you. We ask God to give you complete knowledge of his will and to give you spiritual wisdom and understanding.¹⁰ Then the way you live will always honor and please the Lord, and your lives will produce every kind of good fruit. All the while, you will grow as you learn to know God better and better.

Colossians 1:7-10, New Living Translation

Contents

Contents

Living a Life Pleasing to God

You Can Do It – With His Help!

WALTER ALBRITTON

Foreword

Walter Albritton, better known to many as "Brother Walter," is without question a faithful and devoted follower of our Lord Jesus Christ! He is a dedicated servant of Christ as a beloved pastor, teacher, counselor, shepherd, author, mentor and friend to a vast number of folks who, like myself, have been blessed over and over again by his wisdom and deep insights into what it means to be a fully surrendered follower of Jesus. He not only "walks the walk" of a faithful servant of the Lord, he is also a gifted and anointed communicator of the Good News of the Gospel of Christ who has the ability to "put the cookies down on the table" where we can all reach them through his preaching, teaching and writing ministry.

Through Brother Walter, God has brought hope and joy and great encouragement to countless numbers of people seeking to learn from and live into the fulness of life that is available only through a personal relationship with Jesus. This latest book by Brother Walter is another work of God's grace through this gifted communicator of God's truth!

Living A Life Pleasing to God is filled with wonderful insights and wisdom to help us to learn to live out our faith in a way that honors the Lord and brings glory to Him. It is a treasure map which leads its readers to discover some of the wonderful riches that are in store for those who make it their highest priority and supreme goal to live the abundant life Jesus came to give us.

Followers of Christ live for and serve an audience of One. For myself, the one great purpose of life is to so live for Jesus that one day I will be privileged to one day hear Him say to me: *"Well, done, good and faithful servant. Enter now into the joy of your Master!"* This book gives us a well-reasoned, clearly presented pathway to help us live a life pleasing to our Master.

As you embark on your journey through this helpful resource you will find great help to enable you to live your life in the way Paul challenged us to live when he wrote in *II Corinthians 5:9*: *"...We make it our goal to please Him always in everything we do..."* That is and has certainly been the goal of Brother Walter's life and ministry. May it be the one supreme goal and desire of the heart of each person who reads this book!

Earl Ballard
Opelika, Alabama
October, 2025

Introduction

It has been my experience in reading the Bible that quite often a single word or a phrase will leap out and grab me. One day in June, 2025, it was the word "pleasing" that captured my attention as I was reading Romans 12:1 – "Therefore, I urge you, brothers, to offer your bodies as living sacrifice, holy and pleasing to God – this is your spiritual act of worship."

I began searching for other scriptures which included the word "pleasing" or "please." Immediately I found that it was one of Saint Paul's favorite words; he used it at least 20 times in his letters. My excitement soared as I perused the following passages:

2 Corinthians 5:9-10, Living Bible – "So our aim is to please him always in everything we do, whether we are here in this body or away from this body and with him in heaven. For we must all stand before Christ to be judged and have our lives laid bare— before him. Each of us will receive whatever he deserves for the good or bad things he has done in his earthly body."

1 Thessalonians 4:1, ESV – "Finally, then, brothers, we ask and urge you in the Lord Jesus, that as you received from us how you ought to walk and to please God, just as you are doing, that you do so more and more."

Romans 8:8 – "Those controlled by the sinful nature cannot please God."

John also uses the word: "Dear friends, if our hearts do not condemn us, we have confidence before God and receive from him anything we ask, because we obey his commands and do what pleases him" (1 John 3:21-22).

Other New Testament writers use the word "please" or "pleasing" about 20 times. For example, it appears in this very familiar verse: Hebrews 11:6 – "And without faith it is impossible to please him, for whoever would draw near to God must believe that he exists and that he rewards those who seek him."

I found it also in several Old Testament passages. Proverbs 16:7 is a good example: "When a man's ways please the Lord, he makes even his enemies to be at peace with him" (ESV).

The more I examined the use of the word "pleasing" in the Bible, the more I felt the Holy Spirit nudging me to write a book on the theme, "Living a Life Pleasing to God." I said, "Yes, Lord, with your help, I will." The following pages are the result of that commitment. As I completed each chapter, I asked the Spirit to guide me into a new dimension of living to please God – and He did. I am indebted to my dear friends Greg Lotz and Sarah Olsen for their counsel and editorial assistance. Their support and encouragement was invaluable.

My prayer is that as you read these pages you will rejoice in the consistency of the Holy Scriptures. There is no contradiction in them. There is a divine conformity that constantly reveals God's eternal, unchanging truth. No matter what translation you may read, God's absolute truth remains the same. Some of the modern translations simply make that truth a little more understandable.

The Bible reveals that it is God's will for his children to have a deeply personal relationship with him, so that his transforming grace can assist us in living a life pleasing to Him. Though it is not easy, in this broken, violent world, to please God in everything we do, the good news is that God is ready to provide all the grace we need to live like he wants us to live.

When you awaken tomorrow morning, there is absolutely nothing you can say to God that is more important than this: Lord, your servant is listening; please tell me all the ways I can please you today. He will give you your marching orders, and the Christ who lives within you will give you the strength to obey his commands and do what pleases him. If the holiness God requires is your greatest desire, He will make you a holy servant of Jesus.

Your great inner reward will be the joy of knowing that, with the help of your Lord Jesus, you are living a life pleasing to God.

May the rest of your life be filled with the Lord's divine interruptions that provide for you the grace, grit and gumption to remain on the King's Highway until He calls you home.

Glory!!!

Walter Albritton, sjc
The Cabin
Wetumpka, Alabama
October, 2025

1

Pleasing God In Every Way

*". . . and asking that the way you live will **always please the Lord**
and honor him, so that you will always be doing good,
kind things for others, while all the time you are learning to
know God better and better"*
(Colossians 1:10, Living Bible)

"Pleasing" is a word often used to describe something that is
pleasant, satisfying or delightful. Dairy Queen sells a "Blizzard"
that is quite pleasing to my taste buds. One of my favorite restau-
rants cooks rutabagas and sweet potato casseroles that bless
those same taste buds.

There are many things that are pleasing to the eyes. I have
two sisters; Neva is 90 and Margie is 88. Recently they came to
my home and planted lovely flowers in four pots on my front
porch. To say I was pleased with their kindness would be an un-
derstatement. Watching my dear sisters planting flowers for an
old man was profoundly pleasing to my eyes.

My sisters know that often as the day is ending, I sit on my
front porch and find it pleasing to watch the sunset, as Dean and
I did together for many years. Now, if clouds are blocking my view
of the sun going down, I can enjoy the lovely flowers and give
thanks for the love of my sisters.

Smell may be the least important of our senses, but there
are smells for which we are all thankful. Who is not pleased by the

aroma of pumpkin pie, cherry cobbler, a sizzling ribeye, or chocolate chip cookies just pulled out of the oven? On a good day I can still remember the fragrant smell of the cinnamon rolls my sister Laurida loved to bake and share.

The behavior of family and friends can be pleasing to our hearts. Who can describe the joy one feels when a son or daughter stops serving Satan and falls in love with Jesus! Or who is not pleased to observe their children and grandchildren living with integrity and offering kindness to others?

Some things are pleasing to our ears. The words of others are often pleasing. When a grandchild throws their arms around my neck and says, "I love you, Granddaddy!" O yes, I am pleased! Or when a good friend says, "I love you brother!" That is extremely pleasing.

Music that stirs my soul is unusually pleasing. Some music is nothing more than noise to me. But there is music that puts me in touch with God. Recently I listened to the Gaither Quartet sing "Bless the Lord, O My Soul," and it left me in tears. The song is also known as "10,000 Reasons." The words of this song, even without the music, may touch your heart as they did mine:

> Bless the Lord oh my soul, oh my soul,
> Worship His holy name
> Sing like never before
> Oh my soul, I'll worship Your Holy Name
> The sun comes up
> It's a new day dawning
> It's time to sing your song again
> Whatever may pass, and whatever lies before me
> Let me be singing when the evening comes

I cannot find the words to describe how I felt as I joined in singing with the quartet the last two lines. I was praying. I was worshiping. Yes, Lord, "whatever may pass, and whatever lies before me, let me be singing when the evening comes!" I like to think my singing was pleasing to the Lord.

Yes, there are many ways we use the word "pleasing" in our daily lives, and you will not be surprised to know that the Bible uses the word pleasing many times in connection with God.

King David teaches us what displeases God and what pleases God. In Psalm 5:4, David speaks to God saying, *"For you are not a God who is **pleased** with wickedness; with you, evil people are not welcome."*

In First Chronicles 29:17, David Is praising God in a prayer and he says, *"I know, my God, that you test the heart and are **pleased** with integrity."*

So what have we learned? That God is not pleased with wickedness but he is pleased with integrity. Wickedness is sin; sin is refusing to obey and worship God, preferring our own way rather than God's way.

Integrity is a characteristic of holy living, which results from obeying God. Obeying God produces the righteousness that pleases God. But sin renders us helpless, separated from God, trapped in the darkness of disobedience.

The Old Testament is the story of man's struggle between sin and righteousness, and sin has the upper hand. The only solution is a Savior who can rescue us from sin. The golden thread of the Old Testament is that God has promised to provide that Savior. And the New Testament says, "God has sent the promised Savior and his name is Jesus!"

The Apostle Paul helps us see the role of Jesus in the struggle between holy living and unholy living. In Colossians 1:10-12, Paul says, *"so that you may live a life worthy of the Lord and **please him in every way**: bearing fruit in every good work, growing in the knowledge of God, being strengthened with all power according to his glorious might so that you may have great* *endurance and patience, and joyfully giving thanks to the Father, who has qualified you to share in the inheritance of the saints and the kingdom of light.*

Read Paul's magnificent words again and rejoice that, in Christ, and only in Christ, we may live such a worthy life, a life that is pleasing to God! Glory!!!

Loving Father, grant me the grace, through your indwelling Spirit, to wake up every morning asking you to show me how to please you in every way. Save me from living to please myself. In the dear name of your Son, my Lord. Amen.

2

Pleasing God by Bearing Fruit

"I am the vine; you are the branches. Whoever abides in me and I in him, he it is that bears much fruit, for apart from me you can do nothing. If anyone does not abide in me, he is thrown away like a branch and withers; and the branches are gathered, thrown into the fire, and burned. If you abide in me, and my words abide in you, ask whatever you wish, and it will be done for you. By this my Father is glorified, that you bear much fruit and so prove to be my disciples" (John 15:5-8, ESV).

The Apostle Paul loved his Christian friends in the ancient town of Colossae. Imagine the joy they felt when reading a letter from Paul in which he wrote, *"So we have not stopped praying for you since we first heard about you"* (Colossians 1:9).

Paul went on to explain how he was praying for them: *"We ask God to give you complete knowledge of his will and to give you spiritual wisdom and understanding. Then the way you live will always honor and **please** the Lord, and **your lives will produce every kind of good fruit.** All the while, you will grow as you learn to know God better and better"* (1:10).

Paul makes it clear that living lives that produce good fruit will **please** God. We may learn how good fruit is produced in our lives by observing the fruit trees with which we are familiar.

In the spring, with the help of my son Tim and his son Joseph, I planted several fruit trees in memory of my son Mark who died in January, 2025. The trees I planted are apple, pear and plum trees. I did not expect the trees to produce fruit overnight, knowing that for some time they must grow by drawing nourishment from the soil, fertilizer, water and sunlight. I did not plant the trees in the shade for they must be exposed daily to several hours of sunshine.

In due time, with proper care, the trees will mature and produce good fruit. They will not strain or struggle to produce fruit; the fruit will come naturally as each tree fulfills the purpose for which it is was created. So it is with the followers of Jesus. We grow as we are exposed to the Son, from whose presence we receive the power to mature and bear the fruit of the Spirit. We receive the necessary nourishment for spiritual growth through personal worship, corporate worship and intimate fellowship with other believers.

As we mature in faith, we will not strain to bear good fruit; it will be produced naturally by the life we are living, a life nourished by our connection to Jesus and fellow disciples. The Enemy, of course, will work against us. He will try to persuade us that the eternal God has no purpose for each of us. He wants us to believe we are simply a leaf, here today and gone tomorrow, floating aimlessly on the ocean of time. If and when such thoughts invade our minds, we shall be wise to tell Satan what King David said: *"The Lord will work out his plans for my life – for your faithful love, O Lord, endures forever. Don't abandon me, for you made me"* (Psalm 138:8, NLT).

Like us, David was sometimes uncertain about how God could possibly produce good fruit in his life, a life stained with sin. So he would affirm his faith that almighty God would complete the purpose of his life. He does just that in Psalm 57:2, *"I cry out to God Most High, to God who will fulfill his purpose for me."* In days of bewilderment, I have found it helpful to remember that my heavenly Father will bring to fruition his plans for my life.

Ultimately it is Jesus alone who enables us to bear "fruit that lasts." Nowhere is this made plainer than in Jesus' own words in John 15:1-8 (NLT):

"I am the true grapevine, and my Father is the gardener. He cuts off every branch of mine that doesn't produce fruit, and he prunes the branches that do bear fruit so they will produce even

more. You have already been pruned and purified by the message I have given you. Remain in me, and I will remain in you. For a branch cannot produce fruit if it is severed from the vine, **and you cannot be fruitful unless you remain in me.**

"Yes, I am the vine; you are the branches. Those who remain in me, and I in them, will produce much fruit. For apart from me you can do nothing. Anyone who does not remain in me is thrown away like a useless branch and withers. Such branches are gathered into a pile to be burned. But if you remain in me and my words remain in you, you may ask for anything you want, and it will be granted! **When you produce much fruit, you are my true disciples.** This brings great glory to my Father."

The key is to remain or abide in Jesus, for apart from him we "can do nothing." The good news is that because He is the Vine and we are the branches, we **can** "bear much fruit" for the glory of God!

Are there trees in our fellowship that do not yield fruit? There may be. Jesus warns us that we may encounter trees that bear bad fruit. He says, *"Watch out for false prophets. They come to you in sheep's clothing, but inwardly they are ferocious wolves. By their fruit you will recognize them. Do people pick grapes from thornbushes, or figs from thistles? Likewise every good tree bears good fruit, but a bad tree bears bad fruit"* (Matthew 7:15-17).

In writing to the Galatians, Paul expands the teaching of Jesus about the Vine and the branches. He explains that it is the Holy Spirit who produces good fruit in our lives. But for Paul the Holy Spirit is another name for Jesus; sometimes he calls the Holy Spirit the living Christ. In Acts 23:11, Paul writes that one night "the Lord stood near him" and encouraged him. He was speaking of the Lord Jesus, the living Christ.

Paul asserts in his letters that "living in Jesus" is the same as "living in the Spirit." He warns the Galatians that their sinful nature seeks to control them, preventing them from bearing good fruit. The solution, Paul says, is to *"live by the Spirit, and you will not gratify the desires of the sinful nature."* That is exactly what Jesus meant when he said in John 15, *"Remain in me, and I will remain in you."*

Paul explains what happens if we satisfy the desires of our sinful nature: "When *you follow the desires of your sinful nature, the results are very clear: sexual immorality, impurity, lustful pleasures, idolatry, sorcery, hostility, quarreling, jealousy, outbursts of anger, selfish ambition, dissension, division, envy, drunkenness, wild parties, and other sins like these. Let me tell you again, as I have before, that anyone living that sort of life will not inherit the Kingdom of God"* (Galatians 5:19-21).

I love the way Paul explains that "living in the Spirit" is keeping "in step with the Spirit" – "*But **the fruit of the Spirit** is love, joy, peace, forbearance, kindness, goodness, faithfulness, gentleness and self-control. Against such things there is no law. Those who belong to Christ Jesus have crucified the flesh with its passions and desires. Since we live by the Spirit, let us **keep in step with the Spirit**"* (Galatians 5:22-25).

God is pleased, then, when we remain in Jesus and live so in step with the Holy Spirit that people are blessed by the fruit of the Spirit flowing naturally from our lives. Living in the Spirit inspires us to embrace the attitude of Saint Francis of Assisi found in his beloved prayer:

> *Lord, make me an instrument of Your peace.*
> *Where there is hatred, let me sow love.*
> *Where there is injury, pardon.*
> *Where there is doubt, faith.*
> *Where there is despair, hope.*
> *Where there is darkness, light*
> *and where there is sadness, joy.*
> *O Divine Master, grant that I may not*
> *so much seek to be consoled, as to console;*
> *To be understood, as to understand;*
> *To be loved, as to love;*
> *For it is in giving that we receive*
> *It is in pardoning that we are pardoned;*
> *And it is in dying that we are born to eternal life.*

Oh that the world might be filled with more and more Christ followers who think like that, live like that, and pray like that!

Loving Father, please make me an instrument of peace by sowing love in all my relationships. In Jesus' Name. Amen.

3

Pleasing God by Living in the Spirit

⁵ Those who let themselves be controlled by their lower natures live only to please themselves, but those who follow after the Holy Spirit find themselves doing those things that please God. ⁶ Following after the Holy Spirit leads to life and peace, but following after the old nature leads to death ⁷ because the old sinful nature within us is against God. It never did obey God's laws and it never will. ⁸ That's why those who are still under the control of their old sinful selves, bent on following their old evil desires, **can never please God.** (Romans 8:5-8, Living Bible)

It is a rewarding exercise to study a passage of scripture by comparing several translations. Let's do that, studying Romans chapter eight, considered one of the greatest chapters in the Bible.

Beginning with verse one, Paul makes several awesome statements about living as a Christian. Then, in verse eight, Paul offers this bold declaration: *"Those controlled by the sinful nature cannot* **please** *God"* (NIV). These words beg to be scrutinized seriously. So let's examine several verses in this chapter to expand our understanding of Paul's teaching.

10

We should begin with a very reliable translation; for me, that is the English Standard Version. Other translations are helpful but the ESV is my first choice.

Why begin with a trustworthy translation? Because the more you compare Paul's basic words, the more you are prone to choose the ones you prefer, or the ones you believe will be best understood by the people you are teaching. The goal should be to find the words that best convey God's truth.

The ESV considers chapter eight Paul's insights about "Life in the Spirit" and uses that as a subheading above the chapter. So the word **"in"** captures my attention because more than one hundred times Paul uses the phrase **"in** Christ" and "Christ **in** us." We find that phrase in the ESV translation of verse one: *"There is therefore now no condemnation for those who are **in** Christ Jesus."*

The NIV translation is the same, though the New Living Translation (NLT) is a bit different: *"So now there is no condemnation for those who **belong to** Christ Jesus."* So while "belong to" is a good thought, I prefer to stay with the more common words, "in Christ." What does Paul mean by "no condemnation"? No translation conveys his meaning better than J. B. Phillips: *"No condemnation now hangs over the head of those who are "in" Jesus Christ. For the new spiritual principle of life "in" Christ lifts me out of the old vicious circle of sin and death"* (8:1-2). In Christ we enjoy the peace of embracing God's forgiveness for our sins.

In the following verses Paul says we have two choices about how to live. We can choose to live "according to the flesh" or we can choose to live "according to the Spirit." Either choice involves "the mind." Paul explains that when our mind is focused on "the flesh," the result is death; when our minds are set on the Spirit, the result is life and peace. With inspired clarity Paul insists that living by the flesh is hostile to God while living or walking in the Spirit is obeying God. He concludes this teaching with his awesome declaration: *"Those controlled by the sinful nature cannot **please** God" (8:8).*

The dependable ESV version uses the word "flesh" rather than "sinful nature": *Those who are in the flesh cannot **please** God.*

Several translations tie verse seven into verse eight. This is the NLT version: "For the sinful nature is always hostile to God.

It never did obey God's laws, and it never will. That's why those who are still under the control of their sinful nature can never **please** God."

The Message translation is even more capacious. It is interesting but a bit convoluted: *"Focusing on the self is the opposite of focusing on God. Anyone completely absorbed in self, ignores God, and ends up thinking more about self than God. That person ignores who God is and what he is doing. And God isn't **pleased** at being ignored."*

Like Eugene Peterson, author of The Message, J. B. Phillips translates the scriptures into a contemporary, everyday language. He calls the "sinful nature" the "carnal attitude." Here is the version by Phillips: *"The carnal attitude sees no further than natural things. But the spiritual attitude reaches out after the things of the spirit. The former attitude means, bluntly, death: the latter means life and inward peace. And this is only to be expected, for the carnal attitude is inevitably opposed to the purpose of God, and neither can nor will follow his laws for living. Men who hold this attitude cannot possibly **please God"** (8:5-8).*

Perhaps the best translation to clarify what Paul means by **pleasing God** is what we find in the Living Bible: *⁵ Those who let themselves be controlled by their lower natures live only to please themselves, but those who follow after the Holy Spirit find themselves doing those things that **please God**. ⁶ Following after the Holy Spirit leads to life and peace, but following after the old nature leads to death ⁷ because the old sinful nature within us is against God. It never did obey God's laws and it never will. ⁸ That's why those who are still under the control of their old sinful selves, bent on following their old evil desires, **can never please God.***

Paul continues to enlighten us about how to please God in verses 9-17 of this amazing chapter 8. His words are so affirming and reassuring. He tells us that because Christ is in us, we are alive. We are no longer controlled by our sinful nature. The Spirit within us gives us the power to resist the desires of the flesh and please God by obeying God. He affirms our identity. God is our Father and we are his children! We are not slaves to fear; we are free to live as servants of Jesus. He tells us the good news that because he who raised Christ from the dead is in us, we will wake up in heaven after we die!

Once again, having examined several translations, I must turn to the Living Bible for the most inspiring version of verses 8:9-17:

"But you are not like that. You are controlled by your new nature if you have the Spirit of God living in you. (And remember that if anyone doesn't have the Spirit of Christ living in him, he is not a Christian at all.) Yet, even though Christ lives within you, your body will die because of sin; but your spirit will live, for Christ has pardoned it.

"And if the Spirit of God, who raised up Jesus from the dead, lives in you, he will make your dying bodies live again after you die, by means of this same Holy Spirit living within you. 12 So, dear brothers, you have no obligations whatever to your old sinful nature to do what it begs you to do. For if you keep on following it you are lost and will perish, but if through the power of the Holy Spirit you crush it and its evil deeds, you shall live.

"For all who are led by the Spirit of God are sons of God. 15 And so we should not be like cringing, fearful slaves, but we should behave like God's very own children, adopted into the bosom of his family, and calling to him, "Father, Father." 16 For his Holy Spirit speaks to us deep in our hearts and tells us that we really are God's children. 17 And since we are his children, we will share his treasures—for all God gives to his Son Jesus is now ours too. But if we are to share his glory, we must also share his suffering.

Let us celebrate this glorious depiction of the life we are privileged to live in Christ, and rejoice that our indwelling Lord gives us the power to "crush" our sinful nature and **please God** by the way we live as his obedient children.

Loving Father, thank you for the joy of living in Christ, who gives me victory over my sinful nature. Hallelujah! Amen.

4

Is God Pleased with the Way I Am Living?

For we have not been telling you fairy tales when we explained
to you the power of our Lord Jesus Christ and his coming again.
My own eyes have seen his splendor and his glory.
I was there on the holy mountain when he shone out with
honor given him by God his Father; I heard that glorious,
majestic voice calling down from heaven, saying,
"This is my much-loved Son; I am well pleased with him."
(2 Peter 1:16-18, Living Bible)

Three of the four gospels – Matthew, Mark and Luke – tell the amazing story of Jesus being transfigured on a mountain. This is how Matthew describes this astounding experience which was shared by Peter, James and John:

"Six days later Jesus took Peter, James, and his brother John to the top of a high and lonely hill, ² and as they watched, his appearance changed so that his face shone like the sun and his clothing became dazzling white. ³ Suddenly Moses and Elijah appeared and were talking with him.

*⁴ Peter blurted out, "Sir, it's wonderful that we can be here! If you want me to, I'll make three shelters, one for you and one for Moses and one for Elijah." ⁵ But even as he said it, a bright cloud came over them, and a voice from the cloud said, "This is my beloved Son, and **I am wonderfully pleased with him**. Obey him."*

14

⁶ At this the disciples fell face downward to the ground, terribly frightened. ⁷ Jesus came over and touched them. "Get up," he said, "don't be afraid." ⁸ And when they looked, only Jesus was with them. (The Living Bible)

This is such a strange story one might wonder if this really happened. Peter, who was there, offers in his Second Letter convincing evidence to alleviate any doubt as to whether the story was fact or fantasy:

¹⁶ For we did not follow cleverly devised myths when we made known to you the power and coming of our Lord Jesus Christ, but we were eyewitnesses of his majesty. ¹⁷ For when he received honor and glory from God the Father, and the voice was borne to him by the Majestic Glory, "This is my beloved Son, **with whom I am well pleased,"** *¹⁸ we ourselves heard this very voice borne from heaven, for we were with him on the holy mountain* (1:16-18, ESV).

Peter and the three gospel writers affirm that God is a Person who can be pleased or displeased with the behavior of his children. Since God was pleased with Jesus, we will be wise to ask ourselves: Is God pleased with the way I am living? Your response to the following questions should help you answer that question:

1) Do I need to stop trying to please people and give my attention to pleasing God?

Paul writes about that. In Galatians chapter one, he issues two strong warnings to believers in the church. First, he warns them to be wary of anyone preaching a gospel other than the one he had preached to them. He even says, "Let such a person be forever cursed." Second, Paul cautions them not to waste time trying to please people when they should be striving to please God. He insists that pleasing men will hinder one's service to Christ: *"You can see that I am not trying to please you by sweet talk and flattery; no,* **I am trying to please God.** *If I were still trying to please men I could not be Christ's servant"* (1:10).

Paul finds it necessary to assure the Thessalonians as well as the Galatians that he is preaching the gospel to please God, not people: *"For we speak as messengers approved by God to be entrusted with the Good News.* **Our purpose is to please God**, *not people. He alone examines the motives of our hearts"* (1 Thessalonians 2:4, NLT).

Why are we counseled to avoid people-pleasing? Because people-pleasing indicates we value the approval of others more than pleasing God. People-pleasers will sometimes hide their beliefs to avoid conflict. Their behavior can be influenced by the fear of what others will think rather than what they know to be the will of God. The Bibles teaches us to fear God, not men. Paul's counsel is strong: Strive to please God rather than the devil, who constantly tempts us to be people-pleasers.

2.) What does the Bible teach us about pleasing God? Solomon reminds us that when we please God, He blesses our relationships with others: "When a **man's ways please the Lord**, he makes even his enemies to be at peace with him" (Proverbs 16:7).

In Ecclesiastes 2:24-26, Solomon offers more wisdom about the benefit of pleasing God, even though he includes this in the category of "chasing after the wind":

*24 So I decided there is nothing better than to enjoy food and drink and to find satisfaction in work. Then I realized that these pleasures are from the hand of God. 25 For who can eat or enjoy anything apart from him? 26 God gives wisdom, knowledge, and joy **to those who please him**. But if a sinner becomes wealthy, God takes the wealth away and gives it to those who please him. This, too, is meaningless—like chasing the wind.*

In his First Letter, John says the Lord answers the prayers of believers who obey him: *"Beloved, if our heart does not condemn us, we have confidence before God; and whatever we ask we receive from him, because we keep his commandments and **do what pleases him**"* (1 John 3:21-22, ESV). John goes on to explain what God commands: *"And this is his command: to believe in the name of his Son, Jesus Christ, and to love one another as he commanded us"* (3:23).

No one can read the Bible very long without realizing that God cares about the poor and his people displease him if they do not help the poor. Jesus made that perfectly clear in his teaching about the separation of the sheep from the goats (Matthew 25). As we live out our lives we dare not forget those words that stabbed our souls awake: *"I tell you the truth, whatever you did for one of the least of these brothers of mine, you did for me"* (25:40,

NIV). The writer of Hebrews underlined our Lord's command to care for the poor when he wrote: *"Do not neglect to do good and to share what you have, for such sacrifices **are pleasing to God"*** (13:16, ESV).

The finest Bible verses that reveal how to please God are found in chapters four and five of Paul's Letter to the Ephesians. In 4:17 Paul begins a discourse on "Living as Children of Light." He counsels the Ephesians to "no longer live as the Gentiles live." When you embrace "the truth that is in Jesus," Paul says, you will "put off the old self" and "be made new in the attitude of your minds." This will enable you to "put on the new self, created to be like God in true righteousness and holiness." Paul concludes chapter four with four marvelous verses that show us how healthy attitudes please God:

29 Don't use foul or abusive language. Let everything you say be good and helpful, so that your words will be an encouragement to those who hear them.

30 And do not bring sorrow to God's Holy Spirit by the way you live. Remember, he has identified you as his own, guaranteeing that you will be saved on the day of redemption. 31 Get rid of all bitterness, rage, anger, harsh words, and slander, as well as all types of evil behavior. 32 Instead, be kind to each other, tenderhearted, forgiving one another, just as God through Christ has forgiven you.

Beloved, when we live like that, **God is pleased!**

As precious as those four verses are, the next 11 verses of chapter five are even more valuable. Read them slowly, out loud, and ponder each verse as Paul explains how to please God:

"Therefore be imitators of God, as beloved children. 2 And walk in love, as Christ loved us and gave himself up for us, a fragrant offering and sacrifice to God. 3 But sexual immorality and all impurity or covetousness must not even be named among you, as is proper among saints.

4 Let there be no filthiness nor foolish talk nor crude joking, which are out of place, but instead let there be thanksgiving. 5 For you may be sure of this, that everyone who is sexually immoral or impure, or who is covetous (that is, an idolater), has no inheritance in the kingdom of Christ and God.

⁶ Let no one deceive you with empty words, for because of these things the wrath of God comes upon the sons of disobedience. ⁷ Therefore do not become partners with them;⁸ for at one time you were darkness, but now you are light in the Lord. Walk as children of light ⁹ (for the fruit of light is found in all that is good and right and true), ¹⁰ and try to discern what is **pleasing to the Lord"** (5:1-10).

Paul's wise counsel is built on this great principle: When we walk in the light as children of God, the light exposes what is good and evil, giving us the opportunity to choose what is good and pleasing to God. God gives us a choice: We can live to please him or we can live to please ourselves.

In his Letter to the Colossians, Paul tells his friends he has not stopped praying for them. He explains what he is praying for – "that you may live a life worthy of the Lord and may **please him** in every way." He goes on to specify what pleases God: "bearing fruit in every good work, growing in the knowledge of God, being strengthened with all power according to his glorious might so that you may have great endurance and patience, and joyfully giving thanks to the Father, who has qualified you to share in the inheritance of the saints in the kingdom of light" (1:9-12).

He assures them that God will strengthen them with the "power" to live a life pleasing to God.

We learn from Paul's First Letter to Timothy that God is pleased when we **"pray for all people,"** especially nonbelievers since God desires for all people to be saved:

"I urge you, first of all, to pray for all people. Ask God to help them; intercede on their behalf, and give thanks for them. Pray this way for kings and all who are in authority so that we can live peaceful and quiet lives marked by godliness and dignity. This is good and **pleases God our Savior,** *who wants everyone to be saved and to understand the truth"* (2:1-4, NLT). The more we grow in grace, the more we are inspired to pray for others.

3. Is pleasing God simply a matter of choosing to obey God in all things?

How did Jesus please God? He obeyed God. His consuming passion was to do the will of his Father. The holy scriptures teach us that it was through obedience and sacrifice that Jesus pleased God. The following words of Jesus confirm this:

*"The one who sent me is with me; he has not left me alone, **for I always do what pleases him"*** (John 8:29, NIV).

"For I did not speak on my own accord, but the Father who sent me commanded me what to say and how to say it. I know that his command leads to eternal life. So whatever I say is just what the Father has told me to say" (John 12:49-50, NIV).

"I will not speak with you much longer, for the prince of this world is coming. He has no hold on me, but the world must learn that I love the Father and that I do exactly what my Father has commanded me" (John 14:30-31, NIV).

"I have brought you glory on earth by completing the work you gave me to do" (John 17:4, NIV).

*"If you obey my commands, you will remain in my love, just as I have **obeyed** my Father's commands and remain in his love"* (John 15:10, NIV).

"For I have come down from heaven not to do my own will but to do the will of him who sent me" (John 6:38, NIV).

"By myself I can do nothing; I judge only as I hear, and my judgment is just, for **I seek not to please myself but him who sent me**" (John 5:30, NIV).

"My food," said Jesus, *"is to do the will of him who sent me and to finish his work"* (John 4:34, NIV).

*"Father, if you are willing, take this cup from me; **yet not my will, but yours be done"*** (Luke 22:42, NIV).

All of these verses reflect the dominant desire of Jesus to obey his Father and complete the work the Father sent him to do. The writer of Hebrews offers an inspiring tribute to the obedience of Jesus:

"During the days of Jesus' life on earth, he offered up prayers and petitions with loud cries and tears to the one who could save him from death, and he was heard because of his reverent submission. Although he was a son, he learned obedience from what he suffered and, once made perfect, he became the source of eternal salvation for all who obey him...." (5:7-9, NIV).

Jesus obeyed his Father. And Jesus says to us what he said to his disciples: *"If you obey my commands, you will remain in my*

19

love, just as I have obeyed my Father's commands and remain in his love....My command is this: Love each other as I have loved you....You are my friends if you do what I command" (John 15:10-14).

In his story about building a house on rock or sand, Jesus says: *"Anyone who listens to my teaching and follows it is wise, like a person who builds a house on solid rock"* (Matthew 7:24). Wise counsel, simply stated.

I love the delightful paraphrase of Jesus' words by Eugene Peterson in The Message: "These words I speak to you are not incidental additions to your life, homeowner improvements to your standard of living. They are foundational words, words to build a life on. If you work these words into your life, you are like a smart carpenter who built his house on solid rock. Rain poured down, the river flooded, a tornado hit—but nothing moved that house. It was fixed to the rock."

Yes, we can live a life that is pleasing to God – if we choose to obey Jesus and build the house of our faith on the Solid Rock, our Lord Jesus Christ! May our faith mature until we are able to say, "my daily desire is to always do what pleases Jesus!"

Loving Father, forgive me for all the years I lived to please myself. Thank you for patiently loving me while I ignored your commands. Your mercy has opened my eyes. Help me now to be faithful in my decision to please you in every way possible for the rest of my life. In Jesus' name. Amen.

5

Do This More and More

The Apostle Paul was wise. In his first letter to his friends in Thessalonica, he praises them for having followed his advice. In an earlier visit he had instructed them about how to live to please God. Having heard they were doing that, he urges them to *"do this more and more"* (NIV, 4:1).

I love the word "more." When I was a boy, James Porterfield was my dad's righthand man on the farm. James taught me a delightful use of the word "more." When my mother let me share a delicious dessert with James, he would take the last bite and say to me, "Walter, this tastes like "sum mo!" I knew he meant "some more!" I've had that response to many tasty desserts! My sister Margie's chocolate pie comes to mind!

So while Paul praises his friends for living to **please** God, he tells them he wants them to do it "some more!" Here is Paul's admonition as translated in the New Living Translation:

*"Finally, dear brothers and sisters, we urge you in the name of the Lord Jesus to live in a way that pleases God, as we have taught you. You live this way already, and we encourage you to **do so even more**"* (4:1).

But Paul had something more than affirmation in mind. He had received word that some of them had given up on "holy living" and returned to the practice of sexual immorality or "passionate lust." So he urgently counsels them with these strong words:

"For this is the will of God, your sanctification: that you abstain from sexual immorality; that each one of you know how to control his own body in holiness and honor, not in the passion of lust like the Gentiles who do not know God...." (4:3-5, ESV).

While The Message is more a paraphrase than a translation, the author has a delightful way of "putting the hay down where the goats can get it." His language is not complex but straightforward; you understand exactly what he is saying. An example of Eugene Peterson's paraphrasing skill is his interpretation of what Paul says to his friends about sexual sin:

*"One final word, friends. We ask you—**urge** is more like it—that you keep on doing what we told you to do to **please** God, not in a dogged religious plod, but in a living, spirited dance. You know the guidelines we laid out for you from the Master Jesus. God wants you to live a pure life. Keep yourselves from sexual promiscuity. Learn to appreciate and give dignity to your body, not abusing it, as is so common among those who know nothing of God" (4:1-5, The Message).*

Speaking plainly, Paul contends that only a pure life will **please** God. Those who follow Christ can no longer live like pagans live. Answering God's call to holiness changes the way we live and treat others. This means, Paul says, that as a Christian you will *"never harm or cheat a fellow believer in this matter by violating his wife, for the Lord avenges all such sins, as we have solemnly warned you before"* (4:6).

The Living Bible expands our understanding of Paul's warning:

"For God wants you to be holy and pure and to keep clear of all sexual sin so that each of you will marry in holiness and honor – not in lustful passion as the heathen do, in their ignorance of God and his ways.

And this also is God's will: that you never cheat in this matter by taking another man's wife because the Lord will punish you terribly for this, as we have solemnly told you before. For God has not called us to be dirty-minded and full of lust but to be holy and clean" (4:3-7).

Paul's counsel to his friends is blunt. Anyone who is not following the instructions he gave them has turned away from God. He asserts that because God has called them to live holy lives, "anyone who refuses to live by these rules is not disobeying human teaching but is rejecting God, who gives his Holy Spirit to you" (4:7-8).

Having said this, Paul reverts to praising his friends. Those in the church who had gone back to living like pagans must have been relieved by Paul's kind affirmation:

*"But concerning the pure brotherly love that there should be among God's people, I don't need to say very much, I'm sure! For God himself is teaching you to love one another. Indeed, your love is already strong toward all the Christian brothers throughout your whole nation. Even so, dear friends, we beg you to love them **more and more**"* (4:9-10, Living Bible).

Once again Paul uses the words "more and more," urging his friends to love all their fellow Christians "even more." As we read Paul's counsel to his friends, the Holy Spirit speaks to us about loving one another. Most of us will be quick to assure the Lord that we love our Christian brothers and sisters. But Paul is pleading with us to love them "more." If we take his plea seriously, we must examine what the Bible means by "love."

James can help us. He reminds us that faith is not enough; it must be accompanied by love in action, deeds of love and mercy, for "a person is justified by what he does and not by faith alone" (James 2:14-24, NIV). To say "I love you brother or sister" is not enough. Words of love must be expressed in loving deeds.

John expands beautifully James' counsel:

"We know what real love is because Jesus gave up his life for us. So we also ought to give up our lives for our brothers and sisters. If someone has enough money to live well and sees a brother or sister in need but shows no compassion—how can God's love be in that person?

Dear children, let's not merely say that we love each other; let us show the truth by our actions. Our actions will show that we belong to the truth, so we will be confident when we stand before God. Even if we feel guilty, God is greater than our feelings, and he knows everything.

Dear friends, if we don't feel guilty, we can come to God with bold confidence. And we will receive from him whatever we ask because we obey him **and do the things that please him.**

And this is his commandment: We must believe in the name of his Son, Jesus Christ, and love one another, just as he commanded us" (1 John 3:16-23, NLT).

What does authentic love look like? The question can be answered in a thousand ways. I will share two ways I have seen real love in action. After my wife died, my four sons took turns spending the night with me for two weeks. It was comfort in action; they were saying "Dad, you are not alone in your sorrow; we are with you." For five years they have continued to find many other ways to assure me of their love, a love that has helped me move forward when sorrow said, "Sit down; you are done, old man."

When a man in our church lost his job because of his alcoholism, his wife left him. Unable to find employment, he defaulted on the mortgage payments on his home and became suicidal. Five men prayed with him, assured him they loved him and raised five thousand dollars to update the mortgage on his home. They helped him find a job and persuaded him to trust Jesus and seek help through the ministry of Celebrate Recovery. In less than two years the man had been "loved" into a new life in Christ. When there had seemed to be no way, love made a way.

If we truly love our brothers and sisters, we will find **more and more** ways to love them, and in so doing, we will be filled with the incredible joy of **pleasing God.**

Loving Father, please give me the grace to love others more and more, in deeds of love and mercy, not just in words. More and more, I realize this is the way you want me to live.

In Jesus' name. Amen

6

In All That I Do

This is a trustworthy saying that deserves full acceptance.
That is why we labor and strive, because we have put our hope
in the living God, who is the Savior of all people,
and especially of those who believe.
(1 Timothy 4:9-10)

Nestled comfortably in my memory bank is a song I have sung a thousand times over the years. My pastor, Brother Si Mathison, loved the song; we sang it often in church during my teenage years. The words still melt my heart, especially when I sing them as a prayer. "Living for Jesus, striving to please Him," has been the desire of my life since I first surrendered to Jesus at age 15.

The song is "Living for Jesus." The history of the song is fascinating. Harold Lowden, a composer and organist, wrote the tune in 1915 for a song he named "Sunshine Song." Two years later he revisited the song and decided the tune needed a more substantial text. He decided the title of the new song would be "Living for Jesus," and began looking for a lyricist to write the words.

He sent the tune to a well-known hymn writer named Thomas O. Chisholm who was reluctant to accept the assignment because he had never written words to a pre-existing melody. Lowden pleaded with him to do it. So, with his daughter humming the tune for him, Chisholm agreed and wrote the words within two weeks.

The song was first published in 1917 and quicky became popular. Today it is one of Christendom's most beloved hymns. Six years later, Thomas Chisholm wrote the hymn for which he is most famous, "Great is Thy Faithfulness." What a debt we owe to Harold Lowden for persuading Thomas Chisholm to write the words to a song that already had a name and a melody!

Read the words of the song slowly; reflect on the meaning of each phrase. If you know the tune, sing it quietly as a prayer; you may be led to make a fresh surrender of your life to Jesus.

Living for Jesus, a life that is true,
Striving to please Him in all that I do;
Yielding allegiance, glad-hearted and free,
This is the pathway of blessing for me.

Refrain:
O Jesus, Lord and Savior, I give myself to Thee,
For Thou, in Thy atonement, didst give Thyself for me;
I own no other Master, my heart shall be Thy throne;
My life I give, henceforth to live, O Christ, for Thee alone.

Living for Jesus Who died in my place,
Bearing on Calv'ry my sin and disgrace;
Such love constrains me to answer His call,
Follow His leading and give Him my all.

Living for Jesus, wherever I am,
Doing each duty in His holy Name;
Willing to suffer affliction and loss,
Deeming each trial a part of my cross.

Living for Jesus through earth's little while,
My dearest treasure, the light of His smile;
Seeking the lost ones He died to redeem,
Bringing the weary to find rest in Him.

I love the phrase "Striving to please Him in all that I do." How much am I trying to please God? "In **all** that I do"! Not just on Sunday! Not merely when it's convenient! Not in some ways but in every way, **all** ways! What that means is that I am **totally** committed to doing what pleases God in every way, every day!

At first glance, "striving" suggests that pleasing Jesus is an arduous struggle. But while struggle may indeed be involved in our commitment to Jesus, the word has a much more positive meaning. So let's examine its meaning.

To strive means to try hard to reach a goal, to work vigorously to achieve something. It is used in many ways. A single mom is striving to make ends meet by working two jobs. World leaders are striving for peace. A man is striving vigorously to make his business profitable. A friend is striving to pass the bar exam. The police are striving to make the city safe for all people. To strive, then, means to exert oneself vigorously to attain a desired goal.

Striving can be a negative experience for some people. For non-Christians it can be viewed as struggling, in vain, in one's own strength to reach a goal. Christians may embrace striving as wholeheartedly seeking to do the will of God, though aware that the help of the indwelling Christ is necessary.

We find the words "strive" or "striving" used in the Bible. When someone asked Jesus if those who are saved will be few, Jesus replied, *"**Strive** to enter through the narrow door. For many, I tell you, will seek to enter and will not be able"* (Luke 13:24, NLT).

Paul links striving with prayer when he pleads with the Christians in Rome to pray for him: *"Now I beg you, brethren, through the Lord Jesus Christ, and through the love of the Spirit, that you **strive together with me in prayers** to God for me, that I may be delivered from those in Judea who do not believe, and that my service for Jerusalem may be acceptable to the saints...."* (Romans 15:30-31, New KJV).

In Paul's teaching about speaking in tongues, he gives solid advice to the church in Corinth: *"Since you are eager for manifestations of the Spirit, **strive to excel** in building up the church"* (1 Corinthians 14:12, ESV). The NIV translation uses "try," a common synonym for "strive," and makes Paul's counsel a bit clearer:

*"Since you are eager to have spiritual gifts, **try** to excel in gifts that build up the church."*

In Paul's instructions to his beloved son in the faith, Timothy, he says: "The saying is trustworthy and deserving of full acceptance. For to this end **we toil and strive**, because we have our hope set on the living God, who is the Savior of all people, especially of those who believe" (1 Timothy 4:9-10, ESV).

Twice in Hebrews we find the word "strive." First, there is a warning to keep the Sabbath day holy: *"So then, there remains a Sabbath rest for the people of God, for whoever has entered God's rest has also rested from his works as God did from his. Let us therefore **strive to enter that rest**, so that no one may fall by the same sort of disobedience"* (4:9-10, ESV). Second, the Hebrews author offers this important appeal in the beautiful 12th chapter: ***"Strive for peace with everyone**, and for the **holiness** without which no one will see the Lord"* (12:14, NSV).

That verse reveals God's reward for a lifetime of striving to please him – the **holiness** that is his will for every believer. Holiness is not an achievement – it is God's gift to all who surrender to Jesus, receive pardon from the penalty of sin, and freedom from the power of sin. His indwelling Spirit empowers us to love God with all our heart – and our neighbor as our self. Then, and only then, can we sing with Thomas Chisholm:

> ***Living for Jesus through earth's little while,***
> ***My dearest treasure, the light of His smile!***

Yes, the dearest treasure after our "little while" in this world will be God's approval for our having pleased him – the light of His smile! And along with His smile, the precious words, "Well done, good and faithful servant"!

Loving Father, I praise you for patiently loving me until I finally realized that striving to please you in all I do is truly the pathway of blessing for me. Please hold my hand and help me stay on that pathway. In my Lord Jesus' name. Amen.

7

What Gives God Great Joy

"But his father said to the slaves, 'Quick! Bring the finest robe in the house and put it on him. And a jeweled ring for his finger; and shoes! And kill the calf we have in the fattening pen. We must celebrate with a feast, for this son of mine was dead and has returned to life. He was lost and is found.' So the party began."
(Luke 15:22-24, Living Bible)

The Bible teaches us that *"God created man in his own image, in the image of God he created him; male and female he created them"* (Genesis 1:27).

What does it mean to be "made in God's image"? Since the Bible also teaches us that God is a spirit, it does not mean that God has the physical appearance of a human being. God is a spirit without a body. John Piper's explanation is helpful:

"So I think being created in the image of God means that we image God. We reflect God. We live in a way, we feel in a way, we speak in a way that calls attention to the brightness of the glory of God."

God designed humans to exhibit in our daily lives God's character and his nature, to call attention to God's goodness, love and purpose for humankind. This we do in our actions and our relationships.

Because God formed Adam from dust and breathed life into him, humanity is different from all God's other creations; humans have both a body and a soul.

This gives humans certain qualities that mirror God's attributes. We can relate to God and commune with God. We can enjoy fellowship with God; John describes it this way: *"And our fellowship is with the Father and with his Son, Jesus Christ"* (1 John 1:3).

God is our Father, a Person. The Trinity consists of three Persons – the Father, the Son and the Holy Spirit. The three are One. As a Person, God can experience both anger and joy, just as those created in his image can. God's anger at the Israelites is mentioned frequently in the Old Testament. An example is in Numbers 11 where God is **displeased** with the people for complaining, *"and his **anger** was kindled."* Solomon tells us that God **delights** in justice: *"The Lord abhors dishonest scales, but accurate weights are his **delight**"* (Proverbs 11:1).

So the Biblical picture of God is clear. God is displeased with disobedience. He is pleased with obedience. But the Bible provides evidence that God's pleasure can be elevated to joy, which is defined as "great" pleasure. So in one sense the pleasure of being pleased is good, but less than what the Bible calls joy. Being pleased is a feeling of satisfaction, being glad that something has happened. Joy is an emotion of greater delight, keen or elevated pleasure.

What, then, gives God joy? When does pleasing God awaken joy in God's heart? Let's look at a few scriptural answers.

In Luke 15 Jesus describes a woman who rejoices when she finds the lost coin for which she had been searching. Then Jesus tells what happens when someone repents of disobedience and accepts his position as a child of God: *"In the same way, I tell you, there is rejoicing in the presence of the angels of God over one sinner who repents"* (15:16). Surely the angels are reflecting the joy of God.

Jesus confirms this in the Parable of the Lost Son. In describing the father of the prodigal son, Jesus paints an awesome portrait of God the Father. When the prodigal son "came to his senses," he returned home in shame, hoping his father will make him one of his hired men. The father sees his son coming. He is filled with compassion and runs to meet his son, throwing his arms around him and kissing him.

Instead of reprimanding his son for his sins, the father puts the best robe on him, *"a ring on his finger and sandals on his feet."* He calls for a feast and a celebration saying, *"For this son of mine was dead and is alive again; he was lost and is found."* And, except for the older brother, they began to rejoice!

This parable reveals beautifully what gives God joy – the repentance of a child who turns from disobedience to embrace the forgiving love of his father! We need not wonder what elates our heavenly Father. This is it – a repentant sinner coming alive to celebrate his Father's love!

Oswald Chambers offers in his unique way a further explanation about what gives God joy. He has been writing about our need to have such confidence in God that it is not broken by difficult circumstances. Then he says, "We have been talking quite a lot about sanctification, but what will be the result in our lives? It will be expressed in our lives as a peaceful resting in God, which means a total oneness with Him. And this oneness will make us not only blameless in His sight, but also **a profound joy to Him"** (*My Utmost for His Highest*, August 12). A splendid idea! Total oneness with God results in **profound joy for God.** Yes!

What is oneness with God? It is making our top priority what Jesus called the greatest commandment. Oneness with God happens when you *"love the Lord your God with all your heart and with all your soul and with all your strength and with all your mind; and love your neighbor as yourself"* (Luke 10:27). The word "all" says it all! It means you are "all in" when it comes to obeying God, for Jesus said: *"Whoever has my commands and **obeys** them, he is the one who **loves** me"* (John 14:21).

Oneness is being completely in sync with God's will. It is being fully aligned with God's purposes for our lives and for our world. Oneness with God occurs when you obey Jesus' teaching because you love him, which causes Jesus and the Father to love you and make their home in your heart: *"If anyone loves me, he will obey my teaching. My Father will love him, and we will come to him and make our home with him"* (John 14:23). This oneness, the result of loving obedience, gives God what Oswald Chambers calls profound joy. And I could not agree more!

God is angry when his children disobey him. He is joyful when his children love and obey him. Child of God, let's give our Father joy!

Loving Father, it is amazing to think that I, even I, could fill your heart with joy by the way I love. I want to do that. May your amazing grace sustain that desire within me. In the name of Jesus. Amen.

8

God's Gift of Hope

*I pray that God, the source of hope, will fill you completely
with joy and peace because you trust in him.
Then you will **overflow with confident hope** through
the power of the Holy Spirit.*
(Romans 15:13, NLT)

The most significant thing we know about God is this: God is love. But say that and the cynic will say, "No, that's not true; if God were love, there would not be war, violence, lust, cruelty and suffering in the world!" However, the cynic's denial does not change the ultimate truth: God is love. And the abundant evidence of his love is incalculable.

The Holy Scriptures loudly proclaim God's love. In the Old Testament there appears often the wondrous affirmation: *"His love endures forever"!* (See Psalm 136). The most popular verse in the New Testament says it all: *"For God so loved the world that he gave his one and only Son, that whoever believes in him shall not perish but have eternal life"* (John 3:16). Then in his First Letter, John offers the beautiful words: *"God is love"* (4:8).

The extravagant beauty of nature proclaims in a thousand ways that God is love. The majestic mountains and the lush green meadows declare his glory. Who but almighty God could teach little Hummingbirds to find shelter from the rain inside a lovely rose! Who but a loving God would create plants, like Aloe Vera, to provide medicinal value for his children? Or trees that would produce pecans and walnuts, and apples and oranges! Or flowers whose remarkable beauty amazes us!

If you need more evidence that God is love, think of the times when someone's reassuring love rescued you from fear or failure. Someone whose love could only be explained by a loving God! Or remember those nights of pain and hardship when suddenly you found yourself singing and praising God because you knew that God was with you! Yes, the God who causes the birds to sing for our pleasure is the same God who causes his hurting children to sing at midnight!

Because God is love, he delights in giving us what we need to live with joy and meaning. One of our basic needs is hope. No one can live well without hope. We all want it. We all need it. Paul David Tripp describes well our need for hope:

"Hope is what gets us up in the morning and gives us a reason to keep grinding. Hope is where we look for meaning and purpose. Hope tells us that somehow and in some way things will be okay. Hope keeps us going when things are hard. Your hope is your light in the darkness." (*Everyday Gospel Bible*)

Tripp says God has hardwired us for hope so that our hope-longing will drive us to him. When we give up trusting in ourselves, and turn to God, we discover that God's hope is the only trustworthy hope that will sustain us in our struggle with the common hardships of life. That brings us to the disturbing question of why people suffer.

If God loves us, why does he allow us to suffer? I love the way Paul David Tripp answers this question. He not only writes wisely about hope, he has received God's precious gift of hope in the midst of his own suffering. He confesses the despair that he wrestled with through his physical trials, ten surgeries in seven years:

"Sometimes, all I am able to pray is, 'Lord, help me.' ...It is exhausting and discouraging to be physically unwell. It's hard to make sense of the suffering. I have determined not to let myself get angry with God... I know he hears my cries. I know he is near and active, even when he seems distant and passive.

"My situation causes me to ask, 'Why would a good, holy, wise, and merciful God ever choose for his children to have to

endure such hard things?' Either you quit believing that he is good, or you believe that there is a wise and good purpose behind the hard things."

Tripp offers a good answer to his question: *"Hardship, in the hands of the Lord, is a tool of his grace. He doesn't lead his children through difficulty just because he has the power to do so. His intentions are gracious; he desires that we turn to him and find forgiveness in him. My suffering has produced spiritual fruit that seven easy years would never have produced. Yes, we will suffer, but behind our suffering is a loving God, whose intentions in our lives are filled with grace."*

I remember well a time in my own life when my suffering had dissolved my hope. While out of state preaching in a friend's church, I collapsed during the night and was rushed to a hospital in an ambulance. "A bleeding ulcer," the doctor said. But my dilemma was more than an ulcer. Two of my sons had been arrested for public drinking the week before. I felt like a failure as a father, husband and pastor. Though the doctor assured me I would soon recover from the bleeding ulcer, my bleeding heart had burdened me with shame. The pillow in my hospital bed was wet with my tears. And those tears had washed away hope for my future.

Overwhelmed with self-pity, I picked up my Bible, asking God to let it fall open at a passage that would help me. He answered my prayer! Surely it was the Holy Spirit who guided my eyes to these words in Jeremiah 31:

16 This is what the Lord says:
"Restrain your voice from weeping
and your eyes from tears,
for your work will be rewarded,"
declares the Lord.
"They will return from the land of the enemy.
17 So there is hope for your descendants,"
declares the Lord.
"Your children will return to their own land."

I knew immediately this was a word from the Lord to me. I wrote that in the margin of my Bible. The God who created the heavens and the earth had spoken to me: **Stop crying! I am going to reward your work! I will bring your wayward children**

back to the faith in which you raised them. Now, be patient. I will restore your health and I will give you the grace you need to resume serving me.

Yes, because God loved me, he delighted in restoring my hope. In years to follow, I would recognize with certainty that my hardship had been a "tool of grace" in the hands of the God who loved me.

Think for a moment of your own hardships. You were suffering. Hope was gone. But God came! He restored your hope! You were able to sing with confidence, "My hope is built on nothing less than Jesus' blood and righteousness; I dare not trust the sweetest frame, but wholly lean on Jesus' name."

Then celebrate with me the awesome truth that, when we think all is lost, God is pleased to come and offer us his precious gift of hope. Hallelujah!

Loving Father, thank you for continuing to fill my heart with the hope that gets me up every morning, eager to please you. In the precious name of Jesus. Amen.

9

God Rewards Genuine Faith

*With Jesus' help we will continually offer our sacrifice of praise
to God by telling others of the glory of his name. Don't forget
to do good and to share what you have with those in need,
for such sacrifices are very pleasing to him.*
(Hebrews 13:15-16, Living Bible)

The author of Hebrews begins the eleventh chapter with a definition of faith. It is interesting to compare how the author's definition is rendered in several translations. The English Standard Version contains only 14 words:

"Now faith is the assurance of things hoped for, the conviction of things not seen."

The NIV is also brief but changes "assurance" to "confidence" and "conviction" to "assurance":

"Now faith is confidence in what we hope for and assurance about what we do not see."

The NLT uses none of the above four words:

"Faith shows the reality of what we hope for; it is the evidence of things we cannot see."

The MESSAGE is lengthy as usual but brings in the helpful word "trust":

"The fundamental fact of existence is that this trust in God, this faith, is the firm foundation under everything that makes life worth living. It's our handle on what we can't see."

The Living Bible uses the beloved words "assurance" and "hope":

"What is faith? It is the confident assurance that something we want is going to happen. It is the certainty that what we hope for is waiting for us, even though we cannot see it up ahead."

Having read these several definitions of faith, ponder which one you prefer. Then grab a pen and write your own definition of faith, in as few words as possible. I like to define faith as the unshakeable confidence that God loves us and will unfold his plan for our lives.

The author of Hebrews goes on to say that our ancestral heroes were commended by God for their faith. Then he adds: *"By faith we understand that the universe was formed at God's command, so that what is seen was not made out of what was visible."* "Formed at God's command" reminds us that in Genesis (chapter one), everything was created **when God spoke**: *"And God said, 'Let there be light,' and there was light"* (1:3).

Creation was not an accident. Human beings did not emerge from a swamp. Paul described creation well in his magnificent portrayal of Jesus in Colossians 1:15-17:

"Christ is the visible image of the invisible God. He existed before anything was created and is supreme over all creation, for through him God created everything in the heavenly realms and on earth. He made the things we can see and the things we can't see— such as thrones, kingdoms, rulers, and authorities in the unseen world. Everything was created through him and for him. He existed before anything else and he holds all creation together."

The Hebrews author names several people whose faith God approved. They are examples of the faith we should have. This chapter is often called the Bible's Hall of Fame of faith. The list begins with Abel and moves on to Enoch, who *"was commended as **one who pleased God."*** At this point the author pauses to teach us an awesome lesson about faith:

*"And without faith **it is impossible to please God**, because anyone who comes to him must believe that he exists and that he rewards those who earnestly seek him"(11:6).*

Two convictions are necessary when one comes to God. First, one must believe God exists. And second, one must believe God rewards those who earnestly seek him. Let's examine these two convictions that represent the faith which pleases God.

First, there must be no doubt that God exists. Authentic faith begins with confidence that God is, that he exists even though we cannot see him. We can see evidence of his existence which gives us confidence that he is. For example, there is no better evidence of God's existence than the transformation of Saul into Paul; and throughout the ages God has continued to change men and women into obedient servants who live to please him.

The Holy Scriptures are further evidence that God exists. They teach us that it was God who created all things; that he loves us so much that he sent his Son to die on the cross for our sins; and that he is providing his transforming grace to prepare us for service here and for heaven when we die. So not only do we believe that God exists, we are so inspired by his Presence that we gladly tell the world how great is the faithfulness of our God!

The Hebrew word for faith is "Emunah." It is derived from the root word "Aman" which means "to support" or "to make steady." In a nutshell it means we can trust and rely on God! We get the word "Amen" from "Aman." The word "Amen" is an affirmation of belief. So when we say "Amen," we are saying we affirm the faithfulness of God. He is able to do whatever needs to be done. And we can rely on his faithfulness in every hour of need.

The second conviction that authenticates real faith is the belief that God rewards those who seek him earnestly. It is not enough to believe that God is omnipotent (all-powerful), omnipresent (present everywhere) and omniscient (all-knowing). Each of must believe that God knows our name, loves us unconditionally, and desires the oneness with us that our loving obedience makes possible.

I not only believe that God rewards us when we seek him with all our hearts, I have experienced his rewards. Perhaps you can affirm this with me. You can name rich benefits with which

God has blessed your journey with Jesus. Sharing this with others can be part of your testimony that may inspire inquirers to turn to Jesus.

Three great words come to mind: **seek, surrender** and **serve**. As disciples of Jesus we first decided to believe what God said to Jeremiah: *"You will seek me and find me when you seek me with all your heart"* (Jeremiah 29:13). We sought God and discovered that he had been seeking us so he could bless us. We surrendered to God and began obeying King Jesus. He saved us and cleansed us and guided us to begin serving him by loving others.

That has been my experience. I pray it has been yours also. If not, it can be when with genuine faith you seek God earnestly.

Let's explore the benefits of pleasing God with faith that pleases him. These come to mind:

1.) Assurance of your salvation. Think of Pentecost Sunday. Three thousand people heard and believed the good news Peter was preaching. They had faith that what Peter said was true. They believed. They repented of their sins and were baptized in the name of Jesus. They received the assurance that their sins were forgiven. They received the gift of the Holy Spirit. Many years later Fanny Crosby described the reward God gave them that day: *"Blessed assurance, Jesus is mine! O what a foretaste of glory divine! Heir of salvation, purchase of God, born of His Spirit, washed in his blood."* O blessed assurance! What a reward!

2.) Peace. God delights to reward us with inner peace that calms our fears when times are hard. The peace the world offers us is counterfeit. The world has no medicine to cure the anguish of the redeemed or the unredeemed. God alone has that medicine: the Balm of Gilead that heals the sin-sick soul, the peace that comes from knowing Jesus. When the future seems murky, or your world is falling apart, the "peace that passes all understanding" (Philippians 4:7, KJV) is a gift of God like no other. If you need that peace right now, close your eyes and surrender to Jesus. Ask him to take control of your life. And listen carefully. I think you will hear him say: *My peace I give you. I do not give to you as the world gives. Do not let your heart be troubled and do not be afraid.* (John 14:27).

3.) Purpose. Life without a divine purpose is simply existing without enduring joy. Faith gives us a reason to get up in the morning – to fulfil God's plan for our lives. One of the greatest rewards of faith is God's gift of knowing why you were born. My heart cries **YES!** every time I read Elton Trueblood's inspiring definition of a Christian:

*"A Christian is a person who confesses that, amidst the manifold and confusing voices heard in the world, there is one Voice which supremely wins his full assent, uniting all his powers, intellectual and emotional, into a single pattern of self-giving. That Voice is Jesus Christ. A Christian not only believes **that** he was; he believes **in Him** with all his heart and strength and mind. Once the Christian has made this primary commitment he still has perplexities, but he begins to know the joy of being used for a mighty purpose, by which his little life is dignified."* (The Company of the Committed)

4.) A Sense of Belonging. This reward satisfies one of the basic needs of every person. You know you belong to God. You belong to the family of God, the fellowship of believers. You have brothers and sisters in Christ who will encourage you. They will be there when you need someone to lean on. Because you know you belong to Jesus, you can sing with joy the song that is sung by Norman J. Clayton:

"Jesus my Lord will love me forever, from Him no power of evil can sever, He gave his life to ransom my soul, Now I belong to Him. Now I belong to Jesus, Jesus belongs to me, not for the years of time alone, but for eternity."

Oh the sweet joy of belonging to Jesus – and the family of God!

5.) Guidance. When you belong to Jesus, the Holy Spirit will guide you in the use of your gifts and resources. He will open doors for you, doors you never dreamed would open. He will, as Jesus told his disciples, "teach you all things," and enlighten your understanding of the Holy Scriptures. He will be "with you," not just now and then, but constantly. The Holy Spirit will comfort you and as you walk in sync with him, he will give your life rich new meaning. The more you follow the Spirit's guidance, the more you will enjoy singing:

"Guide me, O Thou great Jehovah, pilgrim thro' this barren land; I am weak, but Thou art mighty, Hold me with Thy powerful hand; Bread of heaven, feed me till I want more; Bread of heaven, feed me till I want no more."

6.) Spiritual Growth. Your faith will grow; you will grow. You will no longer walk in darkness; you will walk in the light. You will experience the continual forgiveness of your sins as you live in fellowship with other believers. John says it so well: *"But if we walk in the light, as he is in the light, we have fellowship with one another, and the blood of Jesus, His Son, purifies us from all sin"* (1 John 1:7).

God's transforming grace will daily change you more and more into the likeness of Jesus, for this is God's will for you. The more you grow, the more you will share Johnson Oatman Jr.'s desire for "Higher Ground":

*"I'm pressing on the upward way, new heights I'm gaining every day; still praying as I onward bound, 'Lord, plant my feet on higher ground.' Lord, lift me up and let me stand, **by faith,** on Heaven's tableland, a higher plane than I have found; Lord, plant my feet on higher ground."*

You will find yourself praising Jesus that you are like clay, and he is slowly shaping you into the likeness of your Lord. Paul describes to the Corinthian Christians what God delights in doing for his obedient children. There is a veil that covers our hearts which is only removed when, by faith, you turn to the Lord and begin living "in Christ." Then, Paul says, *"Now the Lord is the Spirit, and where the Spirit of the Lord is, there is freedom. And we, who with unveiled faces all reflect the Lord's glory, **are being transformed into his likeness** with ever-increasing glory, which comes from the Lord, who is the Spirit"* (2 Corinthians 3:17-18).

O child of God, rejoice that you are being molded by the transforming grace of Jesus into the person God has designed you to be! What a glorious reward!

In chapter 13 of Hebrews the author speaks once again about how we may please God. I believe the author was thinking that because you have sought and found God with genuine faith, and you are now praising God for the rewards he has given you,

42

don't forget to keep on caring for others. These are the author's words:

*"Through him then let us continually offer up a sacrifice of praise to God, that is, the fruit of lips that acknowledge his name. Do not neglect to **do good and to share what you have,** for such sacrifices are **pleasing to God**"* (13:15-16).

So, beloved, as we praise Jesus for the rewards of our faith, let us rise every morning seeking ways to do good and share what we have, until we receive the ultimate reward of our faith: **eternal life in heaven!**

Loving Father, I want to live like clay in your hands. Please continue to shape me into a person of authentic faith like my heroes in Bible. I do so want to live a life pleasing to you. In the name of Jesus. Amen.

10

Faith is a Gift of God

A spiritual gift is given to each of us so we can help each other.
To one person the Spirit gives the ability to give wise advice;
to another the same Spirit gives a message of special knowledge.
*The same Spirit gives **great faith** to another, and to someone else*
the one Spirit gives the gift of healing. He gives one person the
power to perform miracles, and another the ability to prophesy.
He gives someone else the ability to discern whether a message is
from the Spirit of God or from another spirit. Still another person
is given the ability to speak in unknown languages, while another
is given the ability to interpret what is being said. It is the one and
only Spirit who distributes all these gifts. He alone decides
which gift each person should have.
(1 Corinthians 12:7-11, NLT)

Where does faith come from? That is not an easy question to answer. Some people have faith. Some don't. Why? How did those who have faith get it?

It appears that God has hardwired each of us with faith so everyone has faith in something. Some believe the world came about by random choice; some believe in worshiping animals. Christians believe in worshiping God. Is it possible, then, that God has given all humans the capacity for faith and the freedom to choose what they will have faith in? It seems so.

Christian faith begins with the story of Abraham in the book of Genesis. There we learn that Abraham (whose name then was Abram) and his family had left Ur of the Chaldeans and set out for Canaan but settled instead in Haran. The Bible does not

44

tell us that Abraham had done anything to please God. But God speaks to Abraham, calling him to *"Leave your father's household and go to the land I will show you."* God promises to bless him, make him a *"great nation,"* and through him *"all peoples on earth will be blessed."* Abraham's response is quite amazing: *"So Abram left, as the Lord had told him"* (Genesis 12:1-4).

Centuries later Paul writes in Romans about Abraham's faith. Referring to Genesis 15:6, Paul says, *"For the Scriptures tell us, 'Abraham believed God, and God counted him as righteous because of his faith'"* (4:3). Here we learn of Abraham's faith; he had faith *because he believed God.* He trusted God and obeyed God. Paul asserts that Abraham's relationship with God was not the result of good works. Paul had faith. He practiced faith, but he had in no way "achieved" or "earned" faith. His faith and God's approval were unmerited gifts!

Eugene Peterson in THE MESSAGE sheds helpful light on Paul's teaching:

"So how do we fit what we know of Abraham, our first father in the faith, into this new way of looking at things? If Abraham, by what he did for God, got God to approve him, he could certainly have taken credit for it. But the story we're given is a God-story, not an Abraham-story. What we read in Scripture is, "Abraham entered into what God was doing for him, and that was the turning point. He trusted God to set him right instead of trying to be right on his own."

4-5 If you're a hard worker and do a good job, you deserve your pay; we don't call your wages a gift. But if you see that the job is too big for you, that it's something only God can do, and you trust him to do it—you could never do it for yourself no matter how hard and long you worked—well, that trusting-him-to-do-it is what gets you set right with God, by God. Sheer gift" (Romans 4:1-5).

In the eleventh chapter of Hebrews, the author gives us Old Testament examples of faith. Abraham is an example of faith. Why? Because he trusted God. But the question remains: Where did Abraham's faith come from? The solid biblical answer is this: Abraham's faith, just like his justification, was a gift of God. Very likely the beauty of creation and the blessings his family enjoyed had drawn Abraham toward God. The favor of God was all over

Abraham. Yet the Bible says, he had nothing he could boast about toward God.

Abrahamic faith is trusting God, the faith through which believers are justified and made members of God's family. In Ephesians Paul writes about another aspect of faith in regard to salvation. Jesus is now in the picture. Observe:

*"For by grace you have been saved **through faith**. And this is not your own doing; it is the gift of God, not a result of works, so that no one may boast. For we are his workmanship, created in Christ Jesus for good works, which God prepared beforehand, that we should walk in them"* (2:8-10).

Now faith is trusting Jesus or trusting God's plan for Jesus to rescue us from our sins. "Through faith" means that faith, trusting Jesus, is the instrument God uses to save us from our sins. "Saved by grace" means that salvation is a gift of God, a gift that is not deserved and can never be earned by good works.

Author N. T. Wright helps us understand "through faith":

"Faith is not something that humans 'do' to make themselves acceptable to God. Nothing we can do, unaided, can achieve that. If there were such a thing, it would become a matter of our own initiative, and the people who had this ability would be able to hold their heads up in pride over those who didn't. On the contrary. Because it's all a matter of God's gift, there is no room for any human being to boast." (Paul for Everyone, The Prison Letters)

In writing to the Christians in Corinth, Paul includes faith in his list of spiritual gifts. Various gifts are given to believers by the Holy Spirit *"for the common good"* (1 Corinthians 12:7). This is an important teaching. Spiritual gifts are given to build up and bless the fellowship of believers, the church; they are not given so that individuals may boast of having one or another gift. Paul points out that the Holy Spirit decides what gifts each believer will receive. The Spirit gives "just as he wills," or "determines" (12:11).

One translation adds the word "great" to faith. Since all believers are saved "through faith," it seems Paul is saying that the spiritual gift of "great faith" is given to some believers so that each church will have within its fellowship those whose unusually strong faith will inspire others to embrace greater faith in God. Here is the enlightening NLT version of Paul's teaching:

There are different kinds of spiritual gifts, but the same Spirit is the source of them all. There are different kinds of service, but we serve the same Lord. God works in different ways, but it is the same God who does the work in all of us.

*A spiritual gift is given to each of us so we can help each other. To one person the Spirit gives the ability to give wise advice; to another the same Spirit gives a message of special knowledge. The same Spirit gives **great faith** to another, and to someone else the one Spirit gives the gift of healing. He gives one person the power to perform miracles, and another the ability to prophesy. He gives someone else the ability to discern whether a message is from the Spirit of God or from another spirit. Still another person is given the ability to speak in unknown languages, while another is given the ability to interpret what is being said. It is the one and only Spirit who distributes all these gifts. **He alone decides** which gift each person should have"* (1 Corinthians 12:4-11).

God is worthy of our praise! He gives us the gift of faith to believe God and accept our adoption into his family. He gives spiritual gifts, to some great faith to influence the church to share the gospel so that others can be saved by grace, through faith. All of these are gifts of his love! Let us praise Jesus for giving us the gifts we need to serve him well – especially the gift of faith!

Loving Father, I praise you for the gift of faith so that with confidence in your love I may wisely use all the gifts you have given me for the common good. In Jesus' name. Amen.

11

Preaching, Of All Things!

*"Where is the wise? Where is the scribe? Where is the disputer of this age? Has not God made foolish the wisdom of this world? For since, in the wisdom of God, the world through wisdom did not know God, it **pleased God** through the **foolishness** of the message preached to save those who believe."*
(1 Corinthians 1:20-21, NKJV)

Preaching has never saved anyone from their sins. "Whoa, Nelly!" You say. "The Bible says three thousand were saved after hearing Peter preach on the day of Pentecost."

Yes, indeed, three thousand were saved that day, but they were not saved by Peter's preaching. They were saved by God, who gave those people the faith to turn to Jesus for salvation. Doctor Luke never uses one word to praise Peter's preaching. He never calls Peter a "powerful preacher" whose charisma mesmerized the huge crowd.

In the days following Pentecost, many others were saved as the church grew. And Doctor Luke makes it clear that God was saving them: *"**And the Lord added to their number daily** those who were being saved"* (Acts 2:47).

More than three million people were saved in Billy Graham's crusades across the world. But none of them was saved by Graham's preaching. They were *"saved by grace, through faith"* (Ephesians 2:8) as the power of God inspired them to trust Jesus for the forgiveness of their sins.

48

To assert that no one is saved by preaching in no way minimizes the importance of preaching. Preaching, after all, is God's idea. Saint Paul explained why he was preaching when he said Christ sent him to preach Christ to the Gentiles. The apostles understood that they were being sent to preach the word of God, for the resurrected Jesus had said to them in the Upper Room, *"As the Father has sent me, I am sending you"* (John 20:21).

While visiting Albert Schweitzer's hospital in a remote African village, an American tourist was amazed that a man with Schweitzer's credentials would be in such a deplorable place. He asked Schweitzer, "Why on earth are you here?"

Schweitzer replied simply, "Jesus sent me." He could say that because the living Christ was real to him.

I remember well how strange it felt to stand at a pulpit Sunday after Sunday with hundreds of people waiting to hear a word from God through my preaching. I sometimes trembled and prayed, "Lord, please help me; I am nothing more than a farmer's son." But the Inner Voice kept reassuring me, "You are here because I sent you to preach Christ to these people. So, man up, and preach!" I could not run; I knew I had been sent there to serve as an ambassador of Christ. And the more I asked for grace, the more grace he gave me to stay the course!

I struggled to learn how to preach. I wanted people to feel that I was a good preacher, that I could "shuck and shell the corn" and "put the hay down where the goats could get it." But eventually, when people began praising my preaching, I realized that was not what God was after or what I needed. I needed people to meet Jesus in my preaching. I wanted them to feel that Jesus was speaking to them through my sermons. I wanted them to surrender to Jesus and start praising him rather than my preaching. And I discovered that profound joy that flooded my soul whenever that happened.

God loves preaching that presents Jesus to people. And he delights in using preaching as a pathway to salvation. The power to save people from their sins is not in the sermon or even less in the skills of the preacher. That power belongs to God who is often pleased to release his drawing power, the magnetism of Jesus, while a preacher is preaching.

When I first came across the biblical phrase, "the foolishness of preaching," I assumed it meant that preaching was foolish. The word means something that is unwise and laughable. And that was an appropriate way to describe some of my early sermons.

I was delighted to discover that the word "foolishness" in 1 Corinthians 1:20-21 refers not to the preaching but to the core message of the sermon:

*"Where is the wise? Where is the scribe? Where is the disputer of this age? Has not God made foolish the wisdom of this world? For since, in the wisdom of God, the world through wisdom did not know God, it **pleased God** through the **foolishness** of the message preached to save those who believe"* (NKJV).

Paul was teaching the Christians in Corinth that people did not come to know God through the world's wisdom but through what the world called nonsense or foolishness – **the message of a crucified Savior**. From a worldly perspective, this seemed an idiotic idea. But this was the central theme of Peter's preaching as well as that of Paul and Billy Graham – God sent his Son Jesus to die on a cross so that through his death and resurrection all people could be saved from their sins.

The Amplified Bible can expand our understanding of Paul's teaching:

[20] Where is the wise man (the philosopher)? Where is the scribe (the scholar)? Where is the investigator (the logician, the debater) of this present time and age? Has not God shown up the nonsense and the folly of this world's wisdom? [21] For when the world with all its earthly wisdom failed to perceive and recognize and know God by means of its own philosophy, God in His wisdom was pleased through the foolishness of preaching [salvation, procured by Christ and to be had through Him], to save those who believed (who clung to and trusted in and relied on Him).

Leave it to Eugene Peterson in THE MESSAGE to cause us to laugh, and to rejoice, that God continues to be pleased to use "the foolishness of preaching" to save those who turn to the crucified and resurrected Savior for salvation:

The Message that points to Christ on the Cross seems like sheer silliness to those hellbent on destruction, but for those on the *way of salvation it makes perfect sense. This is the way God works, and most powerfully as it turns out. It's written, I'll turn conventional wisdom on its head, I'll expose so-called experts as shams. So where can you find someone truly wise, truly educated, truly intelligent in this day and age? Hasn't God exposed it all as pretentious nonsense? Since the world in all its fancy wisdom never had a clue when it came to knowing God, God in his wisdom took delight in using what the world considered stupid—***preaching, of all things!***—to bring those who trust him into the way of salvation"* (1 Corinthians 1:18-21, MESSAGE).

Loving Father, thank you for the way you use the preaching of your Word to convict me of my sins and prompt me to turn my life over to Jesus. Help me to always listen to what you are saying to me when the preacher is preaching. In the name of my Lord Jesus. Amen.

12

Pleased to Live in Christ

My old self has been crucified with Christ. It is no longer I who live, but Christ lives in me. So I live in this earthly body by trusting in the Son of God, who loved me and gave himself for me.
(Galatians 2:20, NLT)

"God in all his fullness was pleased to live in Christ!" (NLT). Relax a few minutes. Let Paul's words sink into your soul. Try to grasp what it means that the Creator of the universe would pour all that he is into his Son! Does that not explain why we are drawn to love, worship and serve Jesus? The love of God our Father is in Christ, pulling us into his transforming grace.

That is just one of the marvelous word pictures Paul paints for us in the first chapter of his Letter to the Colossians. That glorious sentence, verse 19, is within the awesome passage in which Paul describes the supremacy of Christ.

This is the translation of that verse in the Living Bible: ***"God wanted all of himself to be in his Son."*** Paul helps us understand why. God is invisible. No eye can see him. But Jesus is the flesh and blood image of God. When we look at Jesus we see God. That's why Jesus said to Philip, *"Anyone who has seen me has seen the Father."* Jesus went on to say to Philip, *"Believe me when I say that I am in the Father and the Father is in me"* (John 14).

God was pleased to live in Christ, and he was also **pleased to reveal Christ** to those who sought him. Paul, for example, wrote to the Galatians that God *"was pleased to reveal his Son to me, in order that I might preach him among the Gentiles"* (1:16). And the more Paul got to know Christ, the more convinced he became that the great secret of life is simply this: Living in Christ is the only way to live. His primary message in his letters is not complicated; it is "Live in Christ" and "Let Christ live in you." He preached this everywhere he went. He told the Christians in Corinth that he had sent Timothy to them *"to remind you of those ways of living in Christ which I teach in every church to which I go"* (1 Corinthians 4:17, J B Phillips).

What is absolutely amazing is that God wants each of us to do what he did: **Live in Christ!** And when we do that, we live in sync with God for God is in Christ! Only in Christ can we find the strength to withstand the powers of darkness in our broken world. Outside Christ there is darkness, failure and despair. In Christ there is light, victory and joy. Yes, there is also suffering in Christ, but we can endure it because of the grace we find **in Christ!**

It is no surprise to find Paul saying to his Colossian friends: *"So, then, just as you received Christ Jesus as Lord, **continue to live in him,** rooted and built up in him, strengthened in the faith as you were taught, and overflowing with thankfulness"* (2:6-7). Paul's sage advice to "**continue** to live in him" reminds us that choosing to live in Christ is the first step in the long journey of becoming an authentic servant of Jesus. Whatever your age, you are a Christian in the making. I am an old man now but Christ is still sanding the rough edges off me. He continues to shape me, molding me into the person he has destined me to be. All my life, God has been at work, shaping me into the likeness of His Son. My unending hope is that one day I will be like Him!

I have learned that surrender is not a "once and done" move. To **continue** living in Christ requires one surrender after another until it becomes a daily way of life. It is like breathing; I cannot do tomorrow's breathing today. Each new day I must **continue** to find new ways to be fully surrendered to Jesus, for true life is mine the moment I surrender to Jesus.

For some years I struggled to "follow" Jesus, to "live like Jesus," and to "imitate Jesus," but I found no peace or assurance. Then the sky opened and I saw it: the key is surrender, not struggle. Once I stopped struggling to "be a Christian" and began living in Christ, He began filling my life with joy and peace, displacing the recurring guilt I had felt. The "blessed assurance" I had been seeking was finally mine. I had moved into a new gear: no longer struggling but constantly praising Jesus!

I had a new understanding of what it means to be saved. My mentor, E. Stanley Jones, helped me see what in Christ he had seen: "The cross is the door through which we can enter into Christ. Surrender and faith are the responses through which we do actually enter and become in Christ. Only when we are actually in Christ are we saved."

Who is the Christ to whom God wants me to surrender? Who is the Christ in whom I may choose, by the grace of God, to live? The greatest answer to those questions is the magnificent portrait Paul painted of Christ:

"Christ is the visible image of the invisible God. He existed before anything was created and is supreme over all creation, for through him God created everything in the heavenly realms and on earth. He made the things we can see and the things we can't see— such as thrones, kingdoms, rulers, and authorities in the unseen world. Everything was created through him and for him. He existed before anything else, and he holds all creation together. Christ is also the head of the church, which is his body. He is the beginning, supreme over all who rise from the dead. So he is first in everything. For God in all his fullness was pleased to live in Christ, and through him God reconciled everything to himself. He made peace with everything in heaven and on earth by means of Christ's blood on the cross" (Colossians 1:15-20).

Hallelujah! What a Savior! How remarkable is this eternal truth: God was pleased to live in Christ and He is pleased when we choose to live in Christ! Surely there is no better place to be – in this life and in the place our Lord has prepared for us!

Loving Father, thank you for revealing to me that living in Christ is the only way to live a life pleasing to you. Have mercy on me and give me the grace so to live. In His precious name. Amen.

13

Caring for the Poor Pleases God

*"Then these righteous ones will reply, 'Lord, when did we ever
see you hungry and feed you? Or thirsty and give you
something to drink? Or a stranger and show you hospitality?
Or naked and give you clothing? When did we ever see you
sick or in prison and visit you?' "And the King will say, 'I tell you
the truth, when you did it to one of the least of these
my brothers and sisters, **you were doing it to me!'***
(Matthew 25:37-40, NLT)

As my wife Dean and I made our way into the dilapidated mobile home, a putrid smell filled the air. The source was obvious. On the stove was a chicken neck boiling in a small pot of water. That was all the food the poor old man had; he was cooking the chicken neck for his lunch.

Dean and I had brought in two or three sacks of groceries and she quickly prepared a nice lunch for the man. He was crippled, barely able to walk, and lived alone. We talked with him and learned that his wife was dead and his two children lived in another state. We assured him that we or someone from our church would be back with more food in the days to come. With his permission I turned the pot off and placed the chicken neck in a sack to take with me.

Much more would be done to stabilize the man's life and assure him he was not alone. Our experience that day persuaded

Dean to spend the next few years working with others to develop a ministry for the poor in Opelika, Alabama. That ministry became Christian Care Ministries that continues to serve hundreds of people with a soup kitchen, food pantry and clothes closet. Volunteers from many churches work together to see that nobody has to eat a chicken neck for lunch. They work with the Food Bank of East Alabama to provide food for thousands of people.

Millions of Christians across the world are serving Jesus by caring for the poor. They understand what the Bible teaches about God. That He is pleased when his people help the poor, and He is displeased when they don't. Many scriptures in the Old Testament and the New Testament remind us that if we truly love God, we will not neglect to help the poor.

In Leviticus 19:10, God's people are given this instruction: *"It is the same with your grape crop—do not strip every last bunch of grapes from the vines, and do not pick up the grapes that fall to the ground. Leave them for the poor and the foreigners living among you. I am the Lord your God"* (NLT).

Similar instructions are given for the harvest time in Leviticus 23:22: *"When you harvest the crops of your land, do not harvest the grain along the edges of your fields, and do not pick up what the harvesters drop. Leave it for the poor and the foreigners living among you. I am the Lord your God"* (NLT).

Sometimes I hear someone say about the poor and the homeless, "It's disgusting to see them on the streets begging for help; they ought to get a job and start working for a living like we do." I am tempted to think the same way until I read biblical passages like the following in Deuteronomy 15:7-11: *"But if there are any poor Israelites in your towns when you arrive in the land the Lord your God is giving you, do not be hard-hearted or tight-fisted toward them. Instead, be generous and lend them whatever they need. Do not be mean-spirited and refuse someone a loan because the year for canceling debts is close at hand. If you refuse to make the loan and the needy person cries out to the Lord, you will be considered guilty of sin. Give generously to the poor, not grudgingly, for the Lord your God will bless you in everything you do. There will always be some in the land who are poor. That is why*

I am commanding you to share freely with the poor and with other Israelites in need" (NLT).

The NIV translation of the above passage uses the phrase, *"Be openhanded and freely lend him what he needs"* (15:8). So to a poor brother, we are told to "open your hand." That reminds me of my friend Ken Austin, who champions the cause of the poor in west Montgomery, Alabama. Ken is fond of saying, "The poor need more than a handout; they need a hand up!" Ken's Mercy House provides a hot meal daily for 500 people who cannot afford to buy a nice steak at the Long Horn Restaurant. Ken strives to offer the poor not only bread, but hope for a better life through faith in Jesus.

Solomon encourages God's people to remember that God will bless them if they are generous to the poor:
"If you help the poor, you are lending to the Lord— and he will repay you!" (Proverbs 19:17, NLT)
"Blessed are those who are generous, because they feed the poor." (Proverbs 22:9, NLT)
"Speak up for those who cannot speak for themselves; ensure justice for those being crushed. Yes, speak up for the poor and helpless, and see that they get justice" (Proverbs 31:8-9, NLT).

Isaiah spoke of God's concern for the poor:
"When the poor and needy seek water, and there is none, and their tongue is parched with thirst, I the Lord will answer them; I the God of Israel will not forsake them" (Isaiah 41:17).

When Jesus announced his ministry, he turned to what Isaiah had said centuries before. It is worth noting that the very first thing Jesus said the Spirit had sent him to do was to *"proclaim good news to the poor."*

Luke describes the historic day when in the synagogue Jesus unrolled the scroll and proclaimed why he had come into the world: *"The scroll of Isaiah the prophet was handed to him. He unrolled the scroll and found the place where this was written:*

'The Spirit of the Lord is upon me, for he has anointed me to bring Good News to the poor. He has sent me to proclaim that captives will be released that the blind will see, that the oppressed will be set free, and that the time of the Lord's favor has come'" (Luke 4:17-19, NLT).

When Jesus called Zacchaeus out of a tree and went home with him, the tax collector's conscience persuaded him to speak of the poor whom he had taxed unfairly. Merely the presence of Jesus convicted Zacchaeus to repent. This is how Luke describes the remarkable scene: *And Zacchaeus stood and said to the Lord, "Behold, Lord, the half of my goods I give to the poor. And if I have defrauded anyone of anything, I restore it fourfold"* (Luke 19:8, NLT).

I have learned what Zacchaeus learned. When Jesus is King of my heart, he guides me to deny myself so that I can open my hand, and my wallet, to help the poor.

In his farewell remarks to the Ephesus elders, Paul reminded them how he had used his own hands in the hard work of tentmaking. He encouraged them to do the same so they could help the weak, even quoting Jesus: *"And I have been a constant example of how you can help those in need by working hard. You should remember the words of the Lord Jesus: 'It is more blessed to give than to receive'"* (Acts 20:35, NLT).

Later, in his Letter to the Romans, Paul cites the example of other believers who chose to help the poor: *"For Macedonia and Achaia have been pleased to make some contribution for the poor among the saints at Jerusalem"* (15:26).

All the above scriptures convince us that God expects his people to care for the poor and the needy. But if none of these passages were in the Bible, a single lesson by Jesus is convincing evidence that God expects his people to help the poor. That lesson is our Lord's description of the separation of the sheep and the goats at the time of the final judgment. Read his words again. They have the potential to "stab you awake" and disturb you with the awareness of what awaits those who have ignored the needs of the poor. They will also persuade you to get busy caring for the poor:

"But when the Son of Man comes in his glory, and all the angels with him, then he will sit upon his glorious throne. All the nations will be gathered in his presence, and he will separate the people as a shepherd separates the sheep from the goats. He will place the sheep at his right hand and the goats at his left.

"Then the King will say to those on his right, 'Come, you who are blessed by my Father, inherit the Kingdom prepared for you from the creation of the world. For I was hungry, and you fed me. I was thirsty, and you gave me a drink. I was a stranger, and you invited me into your home. I was naked, and you gave me clothing. I was sick, and you cared for me. I was in prison, and you visited me.'

"Then these righteous ones will reply, 'Lord, when did we ever see you hungry and feed you? Or thirsty and give you something to drink? Or a stranger and show you hospitality? Or naked and give you clothing? When did we ever see you sick or in prison and visit you?'

"And the King will say, 'I tell you the truth, when you did it to one of the least of these my brothers and sisters, you were doing it to me! "Then the King will turn to those on the left and say, 'Away with you, you cursed ones, into the eternal fire prepared for the devil and his demons. For I was hungry, and you didn't feed me. I was thirsty, and you didn't give me a drink. I was a stranger, and you didn't invite me into your home. I was naked, and you didn't give me clothing. I was sick and in prison, and you didn't visit me.'

"Then they will reply, 'Lord, when did we ever see you hungry or thirsty or a stranger or naked or sick or in prison, and not help you?' "And he will answer, 'I tell you the truth, when you refused to help the least of these my brothers and sisters, you were refusing to help me. And they will go away into eternal punishment, but the righteous will go into eternal life'" (Matthew 25:31-46, NLT).

That last statement of Jesus deserves our attention. We who boldly proclaim how much God loves all people must with no less boldness declare the equally eternal truth that terrible consequences await those who refuse to trust Jesus for salvation. Eternal punishment is a long time. Therefore, we must with passion and compassion plead with the lost to turn to Jesus so their eternal reward will be eternal life.

Go back, now, to my opening story of the old man cooking a chicken neck for his lunch. As Dean and I left him in his poor lodging, in our hearts we heard our Lord Jesus saying, "I am so pleased that you took the time to help that man. Remember that I will help you continue caring for my brothers and sisters who need help that you can give. And never forget that when you help someone in need, you are doing it to me!"

My dear brothers and sisters, never look the other way when you see people needing help because caring for the poor pleases God!

Loving Father, please let me never forget what Jesus said about helping the poor. Remembering that will be incentive enough to remind me to do what I can for the poor as long as I live. In my Shepherd's name. Amen.

14

Warnings Not to Displease God

These are all warning markers—danger!—in our history books, written down so that we don't repeat their mistakes. Our positions in the story are parallel—they at the beginning, we at the end—and we are just as capable of messing it up as they were. Don't be so naïve and self-confident. You're not exempt. You could fall flat on your face as easily as anyone else. Forget about self-confidence; it's useless. Cultivate God-confidence.
(1 Corinthians 10:11-12, THE MESSAGE)

There are many warnings in the Bible about the consequences of failing to please God. Paul warns the Corinthians not to take the grace of God for granted. He reminds them that God was not pleased with the sins of their "ancestors in the wilderness," and that his punishment was severe. Because the Israelites *"craved evil things,"* and worshiped idols, *"God was not pleased with them"* and *"their bodies were scattered in the wilderness"* (1 Corinthians 10:5).

"Now these things happened as examples," Paul says, *"to keep us from setting our hearts on evil things as they did"* (10:6). Their pagan revelry included sexual immorality and as a result, *"in one day twenty-three thousand of them died"* (10:8). Paul observes: *"These things happened to them as examples and were written down as warnings for us, on whom the fulfillment of the ages has come. So, if you think you are standing firm, be careful that you*

don't fall!" (10:11-12). He concludes with a reassuring word that God's grace is available to help us resist the temptations that are common to all people.

Paul admonishes the Ephesians: *"Live no longer as the Gentiles do, for they are hopelessly confused. 18 Their minds are full of darkness; they wander far from the life God gives because they have closed their minds and hardened their hearts against him. 19 They have no sense of shame. They live for lustful pleasure and eagerly practice every kind of impurity"* (4:17-19).

This is what you must do, Paul insists: *"Throw off your old sinful nature and your former way of life, which is corrupted by lust and deception. Instead, let the Spirit renew your thoughts and attitudes. Put on your new nature, created to be like God—truly righteous and holy"* (4:22-24).

Paul does not mince words. He says, *"Stop telling lies. Let us tell our neighbors the truth, for we are all parts of the same body. 26 And "don't sin by letting anger control you." Don't let the sun go down while you are still angry, 27 for anger gives a foothold to the devil. 28 If you are a thief, quit stealing. Instead, use your hands for good hard work, and then give generously to others in need. 29 Don't use foul or abusive language. Let everything you say be good and helpful, so that your words will be an encouragement to those who hear them"* (4:25-29).

All of Paul's counsel is based on his awareness that God is saddened by attitudes that do not reflect the Spirit's control of our lives. That prompts Paul to warn the Ephesians not to "grieve the Holy Spirit" by the way we live (4:30).

"Remember," he says, *"He has identified you as his own, guaranteeing that you will be saved on the day of redemption. Get rid of all bitterness, rage, anger, harsh words, and slander, as well as all types of evil behavior. Instead, be kind to each other, tenderhearted, forgiving one another, just as God through Christ has forgiven you"* (4:30-32).

Paul warns the Thessalonians not to *"quench the Spirit"* (4:19, ESV). Quench is an interesting word. It can mean satisfying your thirst by drinking or extinguishing a fire. Perusing the various translations provides the delightful discovery that the Greek word is translated in many different ways: stifle, smother, suppress, restrain or dampen the fire. Whatever translation you prefer, Paul's warning is clear: We must not sadden God by ignoring the guidance of the Holy Spirit!

One pastor's commentary stirred my soul: "Just as a fire can be quenched, the promptings of the Holy Spirit can be stifled. As we read the word of God, the Spirit can be stirring a spiritual fire of conviction within us. Will we respond to that heavenly influence or suppress it? When the Lord is igniting a vision of service to Him, will we quench the Spirit or serve the Lord willingly? When the Lord is calling us to intercessory prayer, will we cry out to Him or suppress that desire He is kindling? Will we allow the Spirit to blaze within our hearts or 'quench the Spirit?'" [1]

Quenching the Spirit began in the days of Moses. Angry with the stubbornness of the Israelites, God said to Moses: *"I have seen this people, and behold, it is a **stiff-necked** people"* (Exodus 32:9). God was so angry with the corrupt idolatry of these stiff-necked people that he was ready to destroy them. However, he relented after Moses pleaded with him to change his mind.

Soon after that, God once again becomes angry with the people and tells Moses again that they are a stiff-necked people. God was so angry he told Moses to take the people on to the land flowing with milk and honey, but *"I will not go with you, because you are a stiff-necked people and I might destroy you on the way"* (Exodus 33:3).

Again, Moses pled with God to go with them. He said to God, *"How will anyone know that you are **pleased with me** and with your people unless you go with us?"* So God relented again and said to Moses: *"I will do the very thing you have asked, because I am **pleased with you** and I know you by name"* (33:17).

A beautiful scene unfolds when Moses bows to the ground and worships, praying earnestly for his stubborn people: *"O Lord, if I have found favor in your eyes, then let the Lord go with us. Although this is a stiff-necked people, forgive our wickedness and our sin, and take us as your inheritance"* (Exodus 34:9).

Many years later, when Hezekiah was king of Judah, he was inspired to *"make a covenant with the Lord, the God of Israel,*

---

[1] **Rev. Matt Albritton, pastor of First Methodist Church, Wetumpka, AL**

so that his fierce anger will turn away from us" (2 Chronicles 29:10). And like Moses, Hezekiah is still praying that God's people will stop being **stiff-necked** people. We learn that as we read about Hezekiah's decision to arrange a great Passover celebration in the temple in Jerusalem. The Chronicles narrative shares how he made his plan known:

*"So couriers went throughout all Israel and Judah with letters from the king and his princes, as the king had commanded, saying, 'O people of Israel, return to the Lord, the God of Abraham, Isaac, and Israel, that he may turn again to the remnant of you who have escaped from the hand of the kings of Assyria. Do not be like your fathers and your brothers, who were faithless to the Lord God of their fathers, so that he made them a desolation, as you see. **Do not now be stiff-necked as your fathers were**, but yield yourselves to the Lord and come to his sanctuary, which he has consecrated forever, and serve the Lord your God, that his fierce anger may turn away from you. For if you return to the Lord, your brothers and your children will find compassion with their captors and return to this land. For the Lord your God is gracious and merciful and will not turn away his face from you, if you return to him'"* (2 Chronicles 30:6-9, ESV).

Evidently the stiff-necked people were small in number at that time so the turnout for the Passover Celebration was amazing. Hezekiah and his princes were overjoyed for there *"was great joy in Jerusalem, for since the days of Solomon son of David king of Israel there had been nothing like this in Jerusalem. The priests and the Levites stood to bless the people, and God heard them, for their prayer reached heaven, his holy dwelling place"* (2 Chronicles 30:26-27).

However, the stiff-necked attitude did not disappear; it continued on. Hundreds of years later, members of the Sanhedrin, the High Council of the Jews in Jerusalem, became enraged with Stephen, *"a man full of faith and of the Holy Spirit"* (Acts 6:5). They secretly persuaded some men to accuse Stephen of speaking *"blasphemy against Moses and against God"* (6:11). Doctor Luke says the men *"stirred up the people and the elders and the teachers of the law. They seized Stephen and brought him before the Sanhedrin. They produced false witnesses, who testified, 'This fellow never stops speaking against this holy place and against the law. For we have heard him say that this Jesus of Nazareth will destroy this place and change the customs Moses handed down to us'"* (6:13-14).

When the high priest asked Stephen if the charges were true, Stephen made his famous, and last, speech to the Sanhedrin. Beginning with Abraham, Stephen described how God had planned to bless all nations through the descendants of Abraham, Isaac and Jacob. He told of Joseph's role in God's plan to deliver his people from slavery in Egypt. In great detail he explained the life and ministry of Moses and how he led the people out of Egypt, across the Red Sea, guided them for forty years in the wilderness. He reminded the members of the Sanhedrin that "our forefathers" had refused to obey Moses. All of this was prelude to the major point of his speech. Finally, Stephen let the hammer down when he said this:

*"**You stiff-necked people**, with uncircumcised hearts and ears! **You are just like your fathers: You always resist the Holy Spirit!** Was there ever a prophet your fathers did not persecute? They even killed those who predicted the coming of the Righteous One. And now you have betrayed and murdered him – you who have received the law that was put into effect through angels but have not obeyed it"* (7:51-53).

The crowd of religious leaders and other Jews were so furious that they dragged Stephen out of the city and stoned him to death. Amazingly, Stephen's last words were: *"Lord, do not hold this sin against them"* (7:60).

The phrase, "stiff-necked people," is thought to have originated with the image of an ox refusing to obey its owner's goad. Like an obstinate ox, people continue to stubbornly refuse to obey God. And God continues to be displeased with his stiff-necked people.

Truth be known we are all stiff-necked, persistently resisting the Spirit until we surrender to the Lordship of the living Jesus. He is not an ancient hero of the first century. He was resurrected from the dead and he lives today as the reigning King of the Kingdom of God. He is more alive than ever, and will gladly dwell in the hearts of those who are being transformed by his grace.

We have a choice. We can resist God and live under the control of our sinful nature – or we can choose to be under the control of King Jesus. Paul explained well to the Romans our options:

"Therefore, dear brothers and sisters, you have no obligation to do what your sinful nature urges you to do. For if you live by its dictates, you will die. But if through the power of the Spirit you put to death the deeds of your sinful nature, you will live. For all who are led by the Spirit of God are children of God. So you have not received a spirit that makes you fearful slaves. Instead, you received God's Spirit when he adopted you as his own children. Now we call him, 'Abba, Father.' For his Spirit joins with our spirit to affirm that we are God's children. And since we are his children, we are his heirs. In fact, together with Christ we are heirs of God's glory. But if we are to share his glory, we must also share his suffering" (Romans 8:12-17, NLT).

We shall be wise to heed the warnings of the Holy Scriptures, ask God to heal our stiff necks with the oil of his forgiveness, and begin to welcome with joy the guidance of the Holy Spirit. Whenever one of us is pleased to make this decision, there is joy in the presence of the angels in heaven and our Father is surely pleased!

Loving Father, like many others I have often been stiff-necked in response to your commands. Forgive me for quenching your Spirit. Give me the grace never again to think I am smarter than You are. Take control of my life and help me to obey You in all things great and small. In Jesus' name. Amen.

15

My Brother

So Ananias went and found the house, placed his hands on blind Saul, and said, "Brother Saul, the Master sent me, the same Jesus you saw on your way here. He sent me so you could see again and be filled with the Holy Spirit." No sooner were the words out of his mouth than something like scales fell from Saul's eyes—he could see again! He got to his feet, was baptized, and sat down with them to a hearty meal.
(Acts 9:17-19, THE MESSAGE)

Saul, a prominent Pharisee in the days of Jesus, was wholly devoted to Judaism. When Christians, after the resurrection of Jesus, began proclaiming Jesus as the long-awaited Messiah, Saul firmly believed the Christians were a threat to Judaism. So Saul set out to destroy the church, arresting Christians and dragging them into jail. Luke describes well how zealous Saul was to put an end to the Christian movement:

"*Meanwhile, Saul was uttering threats with every breath and was eager to kill the Lord's followers. So he went to the high priest. He requested letters addressed to the synagogues in Damascus, asking for their cooperation in the arrest of any followers of the Way he found there. He wanted to bring them—both men and women—back to Jerusalem in chains*" (Acts 9:1-2, NLT).

As Saul neared Damascus he suddenly experienced a dramatic encounter with the risen Jesus. Blinded by "*a light from heaven,*" Saul heard Jesus speaking to him about his persecution of the church. When Jesus told him to get up and go into

Damascus, he agreed and was led by the hand into the town by his companions. There, for three days, Saul did not eat or drink anything.

Luke tells us that in a vision God called Ananias, a disciple in Damascus, to go to the house where Saul was staying. The Lord told Ananias that Saul was praying and *"in a vision he has seen a man named Ananias come and place his hands on him to restore his sight"* (Acts 9:12). Aware of Saul's efforts to arrest and kill Christians, Ananias was reluctant to go, but God said "Go!" and Ananias went.

What happened when Ananias arrived is one of the most beautiful scenes in the New Testament:

"So Ananias went and found Saul. He laid his hands on him and said, "Brother Saul, the Lord Jesus, who appeared to you on the road, has sent me so that you might regain your sight and be filled with the Holy Spirit." Instantly something like scales fell from Saul's eyes, and he regained his sight. Then he got up and was baptized" (Acts 9:17-19).

What makes this beautiful is the word "brother." Ananias could say, "Brother Saul" because Jesus had erased any fear of Saul from his mind. God had told Ananias that Saul was God's "chosen instrument" so that made Saul and Ananias brothers in Christ. What the Lord did for those two men he has consistently done for all who are surrendered to the Lordship of Jesus.

As followers of Jesus we are brothers and sisters in Christ – in the family of God! Imagine for a moment the joy Saul must have felt when the first word Ananias spoke to him was the word "brother." And imagine the smile on Saul's face when, his vision restored, he looked into the face of his new brother whom God had sent to bless him!

Soon God would send Saul, whose name would be changed to Paul, another brother to bless him. In Jerusalem, Paul found that the disciples of Jesus were afraid of him, not believing he was truly a disciple. But that's when God sent Brother Barnabas to Paul! He quickly persuaded the wary disciples to trust Paul by sharing *"how in Damascus he had preached fearlessly in the name of Jesus"* (Acts 9:27). Imagine how relieved Paul was when the disciples welcomed him as a new brother in the church – because his brother Barnabas had vouched for him!

Paul and Barnabas became tight and served as a team spreading the good news about Jesus. On their first missionary journey, they planted churches in the region of Galatia in cities like Iconium, Lystra and Derbe. Later Paul wrote his Letter to the Galatians in which he chastised the churches he had planted there. They had turned to a different gospel from the gospel of Christ that he had preached to them.

Paul felt it necessary to establish his authority for the gospel he had proclaimed to the churches he had planted. We can note with joy that even though Paul was distressed that the churches were listening to people who were *"trying to pervert the gospel of Christ,"* he called them "brothers" – *"I want you to know, brothers, that the gospel I preached is not something man made up....I received it by revelation from Jesus Christ"* (Galatians 1:11-12).

After admitting that he had once persecuted the church and tried to destroy it, Paul explained how God changed him. He is obviously referring to his dramatic encounter with Jesus on the road to Damascus when he says: *"But when God, who set me apart from my mother's womb and called me by his grace, **was pleased to reveal his Son in me** so that I might preach him among the Gentiles..."* Galatians 1:15-16).

Other translations change "in" to "to" so that it reads, *"Then **it pleased him to reveal his Son to me.*** The Greek, however, is clearly **in** me [*en emoi*]. However it is translated, Paul's intent is clear. He is relating a deeply personal encounter with the resurrected Jesus, an experience that profoundly changed his thinking and transformed him from a persecutor of Christ into an apostle.

In all his letters Paul consistently uses the phrases "in Christ" and "Christ in us." So it could be that Paul is telling us that God had disclosed (revealed) his will to Paul by coming into his life in the person of the living Christ. In this same letter he will express this even more clearly when he writes: *"I have been crucified with Christ and I no longer live, but Christ lives **in me**. The life*

*I live in the body, I live by faith **in the Son** of God, who loved me and gave himself for me"* (2:20).

When a person is converted or born again, he or she does not normally experience a dramatic encounter with Jesus like Paul did. But the primary result is the same. True conversion is an encounter with Jesus that motivates a person to repent of their sins, surrender to Jesus, and become a new person who has peace with God. The **old** person under the control of the sinful nature becomes a **new** person under the guidance of the living Christ. Paul explained to the Romans what happens when a person surrenders one's life to King Jesus: *"But now that you have been set free from sin and have become slaves to God, the benefit you reap leads to holiness, and the result is eternal life. For the wages of sin is death, but the gift of God is eternal life in Christ Jesus our Lord"* (6:22-23).

In his New Testament letters, Paul uses the word "brothers" 78 times. The word has become more precious to me than I ever dreamed. I had the joy and honor of having a blood brother for 77 years. He was younger than me and during the last 20 years of his life we became as tight as the bark on a tree. We became truly brothers in Christ, serving Jesus in the same church. Oh how I miss his presence in my life! But how I praise Jesus for giving me a brother like Seth!

In the churches I served as a pastor for some seventy years, many men became more than friends; they were brothers in Christ whom I loved and to whom I was accountable as we served our Lord together. During recent years I have been blessed by the affection shared with a dozen retired pastors in a ZOOM fellowship. They are my dear brothers in Christ.

Some 15 to 20 men have met with me in my home twice a month on Wednesday afternoons for Bible study and prayer. When we began meeting we were friends; over the years our relationship deepened. Our love for each other has transformed us into a band of brothers who are striving to live as authentic servants of Jesus. We meet in what we call "the Glory Room," and God often fills the room with his glory.

The NIV version (and other translations) has blessed us by adding "sisters" to the word "brothers." I like that because I have been blessed with many dear sisters in Christ, including my three siblings for we share a common love for Jesus. Adding "sisters" expands and enriches the meaning of the word "brothers." I love the way John uses the two words in 3 John 1:5: *"Dear friend, you are faithful in what you are doing for the brothers and sisters, even though they are strangers to you."*

Two words in the verse capture my attention: "friend" and "faithful." They remind me of a song that for many years the Lord has used to bless me and my dear brother in Christ, Greg Lotz. The song illustrates how two brothers in Christ can bless each other as faithful friends.

The song is "Faithful Friend," written by Twila Paris. The best rendition of the song is the duet sung and recorded by Steven Curtis Chapman and Twila Paris.

The lyrics have been a springboard for ways that Greg and I have tried to support and encourage each other. We have identified with the opening lines: "You've always taken time to be my brother and I'll be standing by you in the end." It does take time for a friend to become a brother who makes a difference in your life. When that happens, you can truthfully say: "I'll be there to pray for you and for the ones you love" and "believe that He will finish all he started in you."

Other phrases in the song speak of the profound ways a beloved brother can be a faithful friend: "I will be an open door – and an honest heart – you can count on." "God has used you greatly to encourage and inspire." "But I'll be there to pray that He will keep you by his grace and I always will remind you to be seeking His face."

The most significant line is this: "Should there ever come a time to mourn, I will weep with you." That time came for both of us. My wife Dean died and Greg wept with me. His wife Vicki died and I wept with him. In his kindness, God has allowed us to be a channel of his grace to each other. Especially In the hours of great sorrow, everyone needs such a faithful friend.

As you read slowly and thoughtfully the words of the song, pause and thank God for the faithful friends who support and encourage you – or pray for guidance to become a faithful friend for one of your brothers:

Everyone knows you as a man of honor
I am glad to know you simply as a friend
You've always taken time to be my brother
And I'll be standing by you in the end
But I will never put you on a pedestal
I thank the Lord for everything you do
I'll be there to pray for you and for the ones you love
I believe that He will finish all he started in you.
I will be an open door that you can count on
Anywhere you are, anywhere you've been
I will be an honest heart you can depend on
I will be a faithful friend
I am one of many whose path has been made clearer
By the light you've carried faithfully as a warrior and a child
God has used you greatly to encourage and inspire
And you've remained a true friend all the while
So I will never put you on a pedestal
Cause we both know all the glory is the Lord's
But I'll be there to pray that He will keep you by his grace
And I always will remind you to be seeking His face
I will be an open door that you can count on
Anywhere you are, anywhere you've been
I will be an honest heart you can depend on
I will be a faithful friend
Should there ever come a time to mourn,
I will weep with you
And every single time you win
I'm celebrating too
Oh, I will celebrate with you
I will be an open door that you can count on
Anywhere you are, anywhere you've been
I will be an honest heart you can depend on
I will be a faithful friend
I will be faithful
Ooh, I will be a faithful friend

Jesus said to his disciples, *"You are my friends if you do what I command"* (John 15:14). What did he command? He said, *"This is my command: Love each other"* (John 15:17). Our Father is surely pleased when we obey Jesus by loving our brothers – and our sisters. And that love is deepened when we take the time to become faithful friends!

My brother, my sister, let us love each other, sincerely and faithfully!

Loving Father, help me to be the faithful brother, or the faithful sister, that my friends need. Give me such love for them that I can put their needs above my own. In Jesus' name. Amen.

16

Know God Better and Better

*So ever since we first heard about you, we have kept on praying
and asking God to help you understand what he wants you to do;
asking him to make you wise about spiritual things; and asking
that the way you live will always please the Lord and honor him,
so that you will always be doing good, kind things for others,
while all the time you are learning to*
know God better and better.
(Colossians 1:9-10, Living Bible)

My friend Ken Austin invites people to come to his church so
they can get to know Jesus and to know Jesus better.* Paul had
the same idea in mind when he admonished the Colossians to
grow spiritually by getting to **know God better.** In his letter to
"the holy and faithful brothers in Christ in Colosse," Paul says he is
praying for them to **please God by growing** in their knowledge
of God: *"Then the way you live will always honor and **please the
Lord**, and your lives will produce every kind of good fruit. All the
while, **you will grow** as you learn to **know God better and better"***
(1:10, NLT).

This raises the question: **How** do we learn to know God
better? At least three options may be considered: One, we can
look at the answers others give. Two, we can make a list of our
own answers. Three, we can consider Paul's counsel. For our purposes here, let's see what Paul advises.

The four verses that follow Paul's words, *"learn to know God better and better"* offer insight into what Paul perceives will happen as a consequence of knowing God better:

*"We also pray that you will be **strengthened with all his glorious power** so you will have all the **endurance and patience** you need. May you be filled with joy, **always thanking the Father**. He has enabled you to share in the inheritance that belongs to his people, who live in the light. For he has **rescued us from the kingdom of darkness** and transferred us into the Kingdom of his dear Son, who purchased our freedom and **forgave our sins"** (1:11-14, NLT).[2]*

Paul's words cause me to pause with reverence and awe! Read them over again and observe the awesome difference it makes for us to have been **rescued from the kingdom of darkness and welcomed into God's glorious Kingdom!** We are free from guilt and our sins are forgiven! All people, including Christians, must struggle with the common hardships of life. But because we **know God,** we can expect to be strengthened with the power of Christ; he will give us all the endurance and patience we need! Our loving Father has filled us with **joy and gratitude** for the privilege of belonging to his people who live in the light! Glory! Reflecting on a passage like that is surely a good way to **learn to know our God better and better!**

Here is an intelligent question we should ask: **Who** is the God we want to know better and better? Paul offers a magnificent answer as he describes the supremacy of Christ:

*"Christ is **the visible image of the invisible God**. He existed before anything was created and is supreme over all creation, for **through him God created everything** in the heavenly realms and on earth. He made the things we can see and the things we can't see—such as thrones, kingdoms, rulers, and authorities in the unseen world. **Everything was created through him and for him.** He existed before anything else, and **he holds all creation together**. Christ is also the head of the church, which is his body. He is the beginning, supreme over all who rise from the dead. **So he is***

---

[2] **Ken Austin is pastor of New Walk of Life Church in Montgomery, Alabama and Executive Director of Mercy House, a ministry to the poor.**

*first in everything. For God **in all his fullness** was **pleased to live in Christ**, and through him God reconciled everything to himself. He made peace with everything in heaven and on earth by means of **Christ's blood on the cross"** (Colossians 1:15-20, NLT).*

The more you study those verses, asking the Holy Spirit to illuminate your mind, the better you will get to know God! Seventy years ago, Professor Nels Ferre, who taught me Systematic Theology at Vanderbilt's seminary, never began a class without first praying that the Holy Spirit would enlighten our minds as we studied the Holy Scriptures. I have never forgotten his insistence that unless we invited the Holy Spirit to reveal God's truth to us, we were wasting our time.

Getting to know **about** God must not be **our primary goal.** Knowing God better is more than learning facts about God. Our objective must be a deeper **relationship** with God, whom we have come to know **in** Christ. Paul alludes to this when he tells his brothers in Philippi that he wants *to "**know**" Christ!* (Philippians 3:10). As a Pharisee of the Pharisees, Paul knew much **about** God but it was only after he met Jesus that he began to **know** God. That's why he could write, *"I consider everything a loss compared to the surpassing greatness of **knowing Christ Jesus my Lord,** for whose sake I have lost all things. I consider them rubbish...."* (3:8).

Nothing in the Bible is clearer than this: **God wants a personal relationship** with his children. Jeremiah confirmed this when he heard the Lord say, *"You will seek me and find me when you seek me with all your heart"* (29:13). John taught it: *"Beloved, let us love one another, for love is from God, and whoever loves has been born of God and **knows God.** Anyone who does not love **does not know God,** because God is love"* (1 John 4:6-7). Jesus even linked knowing God to eternal life: *"Now this is eternal life: that they may **know** you, the only true God, and Jesus Christ, whom you have sent"* (John 17:3).

Paul teaches us that to grow in the knowledge of God we must continue to live **in** Christ Jesus. And he warns us, as he warned the Colossian Christians, not to be deceived by "the world's basic principles":

*"And now just as you trusted Christ to save you, trust him, too, for each day's problems; **live in vital union with him.** Let your*

*roots grow down into him and draw up nourishment from him. See that you **go on growing in the Lord**, and become strong and vigorous in the truth you were taught. Let your lives overflow with joy and thanksgiving for all he has done. Don't let others spoil your faith and joy with their philosophies, their wrong and shallow answers built on men's thoughts and ideas, instead of **on what Christ has said**"* (2:6-8, Living Bible).

More than once Paul warns the Christians against accepting "the basic principles of the world" since they *"are all destined to perish with use, because they are based on human commands and teachings"* (2:22). Instead, Paul says, *"set your hearts on things above, where Christ is seated at the right hand of God"* (3:1).

The world invites us to find the "good life" by worshiping at the altar of materialism. Get all you can of the world's goods so that your pile of stuff is bigger than the pile of your neighbor. The person with the most toys wins. Paul says that is nonsense. We should **"set our minds on things above, not on earthly things"** (3:2). There is no pablum in Paul's teaching; if our "new self" in Christ is to "grow" in ways that please God, we must **"put to death"** the sins of our earthly nature and focus on "things above":

*"Away then with sinful, earthly things; **deaden the evil desires lurking within you;** have nothing to do with sexual sin, impurity, lust, and shameful desires; **don't worship the good things of life**, for that is idolatry. God's terrible anger is upon those who do such things. You used to do them when your life was still part of this world; but now is the time to cast off and throw away all these rotten garments of anger, hatred, cursing, and dirty language.*

*"Don't tell lies to each other; it was your old life with all its wickedness that did that sort of thing; now it is dead and gone. You are living a brand new kind of life that is **continually learning more and more of what is right,** and trying constantly to be more and more like Christ who created this new life within you"* (3:5-10).

Peter joined Paul in urging Christians to get to know God better, and for the same two reasons Paul advocated. First, so that through knowing God we may receive the power to live a life that pleases God. And second, so that we may be saved from "the lust and rottenness" of the world. Observe the similarity of Peter's counsel with that of Paul:

*"For **as you know him better,** he will give you, through his great power, everything you need for living a truly good life: he even shares his own glory and his own goodness with us! And by that same mighty power he has given us all the other rich and wonderful blessings he promised; for instance, the promise to save us from the lust and rottenness all around us, and to give us his own character. But to obtain these gifts, you need more than faith; you must also work hard to be good, and even that is not enough. For then you must **learn to know God better** and discover what he wants you to do. Next, learn to put aside your own desires so that you will become patient and godly, gladly letting God have his way with you. This will make possible the next step, which is for you to enjoy other people and to like them, and finally **you will grow** to love them deeply. The more you go on in this way, the more you will **grow strong spiritually** and become fruitful and useful to our Lord Jesus Christ. But anyone who fails to go after these additions to faith is blind indeed, or at least very shortsighted and has forgotten that God delivered him from the old life of sin so that now he can live a strong, good life for the Lord"* (2 Peter 3-9, Living Bible).

The more you strive to know God better and better, the more he rewards you with a deeper relationship with himself. It is a relationship that is personal because God knows your name and you know him by virtue of your new birth. Remember how Jesus affirmed a personal relationship with him: *"I am the good shepherd; I know my sheep and **my sheep know me"*** (John 10:14).

By living in Christ we learn **the power to live a holy life** is not ours; it is his power flowing into us, as the power of the vine flows into the branches. Christ give us the "knowledge" we need to know his will and the awareness that only by abiding in him can we know and do his will. The primary source of our knowledge is the Bible. As we study God's word, and grow spiritually, we gain a better understanding of the ways and will of God.

We shall be wise to assume Peter was speaking to us when he warned his readers to guard against what Paul called the principles of the world and urged them to continue growing in grace and in the knowledge of Christ:

"You already know these things, dear friends. So be on guard; then you will not be carried away by the errors of these

*wicked people and lose your own secure footing. Rather, **you must grow in the grace and knowledge of our Lord** and Savior Jesus Christ. All glory to him, both now and forever! Amen"* (2 Peter 3:17-18, NLT).

Pause, for a "smell the roses moment," and praise God that you may "grow in the grace and knowledge of our Lord," and enjoy a deeply personal relationship with your loving, heavenly Father. He knows you well; he wants you to know him better.

Loving Father, that you love me and know my name thrills my soul. Forgive me for not spending more time listening to you. I do so want to know You better. Fill me with your Holy Spirit so that, like Paul, I will value nothing more than knowing you and obeying you. Today I surrender to the goal of knowing you better and better for the rest of my life. In the name of Jesus, my Lord and Savior. Amen.

17

Fix Your Eyes On the Unseen

*So we fix our eyes not on what is seen, but on what is unseen,
since what is seen is temporary, but what is unseen is eternal.*
(2 Corinthians 4:18)

At first glance Paul's assertion that his eyes were focused on "what is unseen" may have seemed foolish to his friends in Corinth. But the Holy Scriptures confirm Paul's wisdom about the temporary and the eternal. Indeed, if we are to live a life pleasing to God, we must embrace Paul's truth and fix our gaze on the unseen, not on what is seen.

Earthly things deceive us. We imagine material things will bring us joy only to discover they do not and cannot, for our spiritual nature desires something that cannot be seen — a personal relationship with God that brings joy, peace and meaning into our lives.

In Psalm 49, David warns us against the deceptive nature of money and the foolishness of *"trusting in wealth and boasting of great riches"* (49:6). He reminds us that both the wise and the foolish will die "and leave their wealth to others" (49:10). Only God can redeem us, and take us to himself, David says, so we should *"not be overawed when a man grows rich, when the splendor of his house increases, for he will take nothing with him when he dies...."* (49:16-17). The concluding verse conveys a sobering truth: *"A man who has riches without understanding is like the beasts that perish"* (49:20).

Central to the Christian faith is God's expectation that his people will forsake worshiping the temporary and worship the unseen reality of the spiritual world. Faith itself is the assurance that what we hope for, the things we cannot see, are real, more real than things you can touch. If you have difficulty, as many do, in believing the unseen is real, consider the trust of your spouse. You cannot see it, but when you know you have it, it is truly **real** though unseen. And like the unseen love of God, it is a precious gift! Authentic faith is trusting God that what we believe is true without any observable evidence to prove it.

Paul wrote of "walking by faith," instead of walking by what can be seen with physical eyes. With his steady focus on the eternal, Paul "saw" the unseen – the day when each of us will stand before the judgment seat of Christ. And, in the meantime, Paul said, our focus must be on **pleasing** the Lord:

*"So we are always of good courage. We know that while we are at home in the body we are away from the Lord, for **we walk by faith, not by sight**. Yes, we are of good courage, and we would rather be away from the body and at home with the Lord. So whether we are at home or away, we make it **our aim to please him.** For we must all appear before the judgment seat of Christ, so that each one may receive what is due for what he has done in the body, whether good or evil"* (2 Corinthians 5:6-10, ESV).

Such faith in the unseen requires "eyes of faith," eyes of the heart, eyes of the soul. Most of us spend too much time looking at ourselves, "fixing our face," so that others will think well of us. It would be wise to spend more time asking Jesus to "fix" our heart. The writer of Hebrews invites us to take our eyes off of ourselves and fix them unwaveringly on Jesus: *"And let us run with endurance the race God has set before us. We do this **by keeping our eyes on Jesus,** the champion who initiates and perfects our faith. Because of the joy awaiting him, he endured the cross, disregarding its shame"* (12:1-2).

The world wants us to believe we need fancy, expensive clothes so others will admire us. Paul, however, never mentions

81

needing a new suit. He did recommend clothes that Christians should wear:

"Since God chose you to be the holy people he loves, you must **clothe yourselves** *with tenderhearted mercy, kindness, humility, gentleness, and patience. Make allowance for each other's faults, and forgive anyone who offends you. Remember, the Lord forgave you, so you must forgive others. Above all,* **clothe yourselves with love***, which binds us all together in perfect harmony."* (Colossians 3:12-14, NLT).

Paul never asked his friends to help him raise the money to purchase a nice home on some lake so he could go there and relax from the persecution of those who opposed his ministry. He never urged any church to help him raise funds to purchase a new horse, a new suit, or a Yamaha WaveRunner for his excursions on the Sea of Galilee. Instead, he wrote memorable words about an unseen reality called love:

"If I could speak all the languages of earth and of angels, but didn't love others, I would only be a noisy gong or a clanging cymbal. If I had the gift of prophecy, and if I understood all of God's secret plans and possessed all knowledge, and if I had such faith that I could move mountains, but didn't love others, I would be nothing. If I gave everything I have to the poor and even sacrificed my body, I could boast about it but if I didn't love others, I would have gained nothing.

"Love is patient and kind. Love is not jealous or boastful or proud or rude. It does not demand its own way. It is not irritable, and it keeps no record of being wronged. It does not rejoice about injustice but rejoices whenever the truth wins out. Love never gives up, never loses faith, is always hopeful, and endures through every circumstance" (1 Corinthians 13:1-7, NLT).

A home on the lake is temporary. Our satisfaction with the "toys" of men and boys (and girls!) is here today and gone tomorrow. The love of which Paul writes so eloquently is eternal. The pleasure of the temporary lasts for a little while; the joy of the unseen lasts forever.

Jesus warns us against thinking that life can be measured by the things we own: *"Watch out! Be on your guard against all kinds of greed; a man's life does not consist in the abundance of his possessions"* (Luke 12:15). The Living Bible translation is different but helpful: *"Beware! Don't always be wishing for what you don't have. For real life and real living are not related to how rich we are."*

Our Lord Jesus even advised his disciples not to store up earthly treasures but to store treasures in heaven:

"Don't store up treasures here on earth, where moths eat them and rust destroys them, and where thieves break in and steal. Store your treasures in heaven, where moths and rust cannot destroy, and thieves do not break in and steal. Wherever your treasure is, there the desires of your heart will also be"
(Matthew 6:19-21, NLT).

Are Christians who take Jesus seriously and find ways to store treasures in heaven guilty of naïve optimism? Some people think so. Joe Hill did. Hill was a Swedish-American labor activist in Portland, Oregon, who expressed his ridicule for "long-haired preachers" in a song he wrote in 1910 titled "The Preacher and the Slave." Hill gave us the phrase "pie in the sky."

In his song he accused the long-haired preachers of the Salvation Army of telling workers not to worry about their earthly needs because they would soon be eating pie in the sky bye and bye. He wrote his song to the tune of the popular gospel song, "In the Sweet By-and-By" by Joseph Webster. Here are the pathetic words of Hill's ridicule and his unfair criticism of the Salvation Army preachers:

Long-haired preachers come out every night
Try to tell you what's wrong and what's right
But when asked about something to eat
They will answer in voices so sweet
CHORUS:
You will eat, bye and bye
In that glorious land above the sky
Work and pray, live on hay
You'll get pie in the sky when you die (that's a lie)
And the starvation army they play
And they sing and they clap and they pray

Till they get all your coin on the drum
Then they tell you when you're on the bum
Holy rollers and jumpers come out
They holler, they jump, and they shout
Give your money to Jesus they say
He will cure all diseases today
If you fight hard for children and wife
Try to get something good in this life
You're a sinner and bad man, they tell
When you die you will sure go to hell
Workingmen (folk) of all countries unite
Side by side we for freedom will fight
When the world and its wealth we have gained
To the grafters we'll sing this refrain
LAST CHORUS:
You will eat, bye and bye
When you've learned how to cook and to fry
Chop some wood, twill do you good
And you'll eat in the sweet bye and bye (that's no lie)

Joe Hill became a folk hero by fighting for labor rights and racial equality but he failed to see the unseen. His gaze was totally on what could be seen. He was right in caring for the ordinary working man or woman, but he was wrong in his world view. Biblically speaking, Hill was blind; he never asked Jesus to open his eyes so he could see "the land that is fairer than day." Joseph Webster saw it and his melodic vision inspires God's people to gaze at the unseen Webster described so well:

There's a land that is fairer than day,
And by faith we can see it afar,
For the Father waits over the way
To prepare us a dwelling place there.
Refrain:
In the sweet by and by,
We shall meet on that beautiful shore;
In the sweet by and by,
We shall meet on that beautiful shore.

We shall sing on that beautiful shore
The melodious songs of the blest;
And our spirits shall sorrow no more-
Not a sigh for the blessing of rest.
To our bountiful Father above
We will offer our tribute of praise
For the glorious gift of His love
And the blessings that hallow our days.

C. S. Lewis saw that beautiful shore "where our spirits shall sorrow no more." He had the faith to "see it afar," which led him to declare, "If I find in myself desires which nothing in this world can satisfy, the only logical explanation is that I was made for another world."

Those desires that nothing in this world can satisfy can only be satisfied by fixing our eyes on the unseen. When we choose to do that, we can with the eyes of faith join with Paul in saying to those who think the temporary is all there is:

"So we don't look at the troubles we can see now; rather, we fix our gaze on things that cannot be seen. For the things we see now will soon be gone, but the things we cannot see will last forever" (2 Corinthians 4:18, NLT).

Loving Father, I confess that I look too much at temporary things. Forgive me and help me to fix my eyes on the eternal things that will last forever. Most of all, help me to only glance at my problems but gaze unwaveringly at my Lord Jesus Christ so that my daily life will be filled with obedience to His will. In His dear name. Amen.

18

God's Will — A Holy Life Pleasing to God

*⁴ Finally, then, brothers and sisters, we ask and urge you in the
Lord Jesus, that as you received from us how you ought to walk
and **to please God**, just as you are doing, that you do so more
and more. ² For you know what instructions we gave you through
the Lord Jesus. ³ For **this is the will of God, your sanctification**:
that you abstain from sexual immorality; ⁴ that each one of you
know how to control his own body **in holiness and honor**, ⁵ not in
the passion of lust like the Gentiles who do not know God; ⁶ that no
one transgress and wrong his brother in this matter, because the
Lord is an avenger in all these things, as we told you beforehand
and solemnly warned you. ⁷ For God has not called us for impurity,
but in **holiness**.⁸ Therefore whoever disregards this, disregards
not man but God, who gives his Holy Spirit to you.*
(1 Thessalonians 4:1-8, ESV)

The Apostle Paul affirmed the Thessalonian Christians for following his instructions about how to live in order to please God.
He urged them keep on doing what they had been doing but to do
it "more and more." He goes on to assert that sanctification is
God's will, *"for God did not call us to be impure, but to **live a holy
life**"* (1 Thessalonians 4:7).

The word "sanctification" is a red flag for many believers who were never taught its meaning or confronted with God's expectation that his people should live holy lives, having been set free from the power of sin. It is rather surprising that this describes many Methodists since "entire sanctification" was a core belief of John Wesley, the founder of Methodism.

Wesley called entire sanctification "Christian Perfection," which he insisted was scriptural Christianity. The basic idea is that the full salvation Christ offers us is not only forgiveness of past sins but also freedom from the power of sin in the present life. Christians, Wesley taught, can by the grace of God be made holy in their lifetime and empowered by the Holy Spirit to love God and their neighbors perfectly. For Wesley, perfect love was not a human achievement but a work of God in the heart of those whose passionate desire is to obey and please God. The believer is "perfected in love," but this does not mean that he has achieved sinless perfection.

Over the years the Methodists for the most part have neglected to teach and preach entire sanctification. The result has been ignorance in the ranks of Methodist Christians. This is most disturbing since John Wesley believed God raised up the Methodists to strengthen Christianity with this doctrine. Not long before Wesley died, in a letter to a friend, he described entire sanctification as "the grand depositum which God has lodged with the people called Methodists; and for the sake of propagating this chiefly He appeared to have raised us up."

The good news is that many voices in Methodism across the world are calling for a return to the teaching of this vital doctrine. Two recent books by Methodist leaders have been well received. Each author has issued a passionate challenge to recover and propagate Wesley's core belief and experience the holiness that awaits those who surrender to Jesus and ask God to make them holy.

Kevin M. Watson, in his book, *Perfect Love, Recovering Entire Sanctification—The Lost Power of the Methodist Movement*, (published by Seedbed) says:

"Methodism is in the midst of an identity crisis. We have forgotten who we are. We have abandoned our theological heritage."

Watson asserts: "Above all else, God raised up the people called Methodists to preach, teach, and experience one core doctrine. This doctrine is Methodism's reason for existence. If we get this right, everything else will fall into place. If we get it wrong, we will miss the unique calling and purpose that God has for us."

Watson explains clearly what entire sanctification is, and what it is not. And he offers an excellent explanation about how to receive entire sanctification today. I love Watson's emphasis on the place of Jesus in experience of salvation:

"Jesus is at the center of the Christian understanding of salvation. Jesus makes forgiveness and pardon with God for sin possible. We can approach God the Father with confidence that we will receive what we do not deserve (grace, forgiveness, and healing) because of the work Jesus has done for us. Jesus makes it possible for us to not only be forgiven, but also to be empowered to live lives of joyful obedience and faithfulness to God."

The second influential book for Methodists is by a pastor, Matt O'Reilly, titled *Free to Be Holy, A Biblical Theology of Sanctification*, also published by *Seedbed.* Matt offers brilliant answers to these two questions: What is holiness? and How holy can we be?

"Holiness is a life turned away from self-interest and marked by love for God and your neighbor (and enemy). Holiness doesn't mean we won't experience temptation. It doesn't mean we won't sin. It does mean we don't have to sin when tempted. Instead of choosing to chase after sin, the Holy Spirit who dwells in us can enable us to choose to chase after God. This is God's purpose for us. Sin and self-interest rob us of experiencing God's best for us. Jesus offers so much more. He offers healing, fullness, restoration, wholeness, and holiness. He offers a life of perfect love."

Matt answers the second question by reminding us that "God has promised to cleanse his people of **all** their idols. God has declared his desire to sanctify you **entirely.** God is able to bring his love to **perfection** in you. The consistent testimony of Scripture – Old Testament and New Testament – is that God's will for you is holiness, not partial holiness, but full holiness. So, what can you expect? Expect him to do what he has promised to do. Expect him to cleanse you and to cleanse you fully. Expect him to bring his love to perfection in your life. Don't strive for it. Surrender to it. 'The one who calls you is faithful, and he will do this.' (1 Thess. 5:24)."

Over many years Oswald Chambers has mentored me about entire sanctification through his book, *My Utmost for His Highest*. He calls sanctification "God's second mighty work of grace." Here are a few of his helpful teachings on holiness:

"In sanctification, the one who has been born again deliberately gives up his right to himself to Jesus Christ, and identifies himself entirely with God's ministry to others."

"No one experiences complete sanctification without going through a 'white funeral' – the burial of the old life."

"Sanctification means being made one with Jesus so that the nature that controlled Him will control us....It will cost absolutely everything in us that is not of God....The resounding evidence of the Holy Spirit in a person's life is the unmistakable likeness to Jesus Christ, and the freedom from everything which is not like Him."

"When I pray, 'Lord, show me what sanctification means for me,' He will show me. It means being made one with Jesus. Sanctification is not something Jesus puts in me – it is *Himself* in me (see 1 Corinthians 1:30)."

"Once God has begun the process of sanctification in your life, watch and see how God causes your confidence in your own natural virtues and power to wither away. He will continue until you learn how to draw your life from the reservoir of the resurrection life of Jesus. Thank God if you are going through this drying-up experience!"

Chambers' insights have been of immeasurable value to me in understanding how to pursue the holiness that God expects of me, and of every child of God.

If you have not yet experienced the sanctifying power of the Holy Spirit in your life, I pray that, after reading the above, you have become hungry for it. Remember that it is futile to strive to be holy. When you truly desire for God to make you holy, the first step is to surrender fully to Jesus and ask Him to do for you what you cannot do for yourself. Let God know that your greatest desire is to obey and please Him. Open your entire life to the life-changing power of the Spirit. Kevin Watson says that what we seek is ours only when we "receive" it from God:

"We only experience the fullness of the love, joy, and peace that God intends for us when we receive power from God to walk in freedom, in purity, and in harmony with God's will."

Watson says, "Those who have gone before us, those who have received Wesley's grand depositum, testify to joy and intimacy with the Lord and a soul that is at rest because it abides in the perfect love of God given us in Christ Jesus."

It is God's will for you to be sanctified. He wants His love to be perfected in you. He is ready and willing to sanctify you entirely. When you are ready, and completely willing for God to sanctify you, you can pray this prayer:

Loving Father, I have received your forgiveness for my sins, but I want more. I want all that you want me to have. I know I cannot achieve a holy life, but I am hungry for the gift of your perfect love so I may live a holy life pleasing to you. In this moment I surrender my life to you as fully as I know how, and I ask you to sanctify me entirely, by the power of your Holy Spirit, for the sake of your Son, my Lord Jesus. Amen.

19

"But the Lord"

*He died for all so that all who live—having received eternal life
from him—might live no longer for themselves, to please
themselves, but to **spend their lives pleasing Christ** who died
and rose again for them. So stop evaluating Christians by what the
world thinks about them or by what they seem to be like on the
outside. Once I mistakenly thought of Christ that way, merely as a
human being like myself. How differently I feel now! When
someone becomes a Christian, he becomes a brand-new person
inside. He is not the same anymore. A new life has begun!*
(2 Corinthians 5:15-18, Living Bible)

This year I am reading daily the Everyday Gospel Bible, which
includes a brief commentary on each book and a prayer by the
General Editor, Paul David Tripp. In his summary of the Book of
Jonah, Tripp surprised me by saying that three words in this small
book, *"But the Lord,"* (Jonah 1:4, ESV) are three of the most important words ever written. Tripp says these words are important because they "have the power to change us and everything about us." As I read Tripp's assertions, the Holy Spirit said
to me, "Those three words would be a great title for this chapter
about the life-changing power of God." Joyfully, I said, "Yes, Lord!
Thank you! I got it!"

Tripp calls what happened to Jonah a "divine interruption." I love that because it has been the Lord's divine interruptions that have changed my own life. I believe Tripp's appraisal of
the Book of Jonah will bless you as they blessed me:

91

"In these words, as God interrupts our story to embed us in his story, we find our hope as well. Without these words there would be no covenant promises, no Bible, no coming of Christ, no church, no conviction in our hearts, no ability to believe. Without these words there would be no protecting, providing, delivering, transforming grace. Our life hangs on these three words: 'But the Lord.' If Jonah were only three words long, 'But the Lord,' it would still have a valuable place in the great Old Testament narrative" (*Everyday Gospel Bible*, page 1166).

Once living to please God becomes your primary goal, you will experience God's divine interruptions that will change everything about you. The change will be mostly gradual, and possibly dramatic sometimes, in every aspect of your life. Your values will change. Your behavior will change. Your goals will change. Your attitudes will change. Why? Because choosing to please God means that you have surrendered to the control of the Holy Spirit. And that's when you will begin to understand what "But the Lord" means in your own life.

The Bible speaks of the "old man" and the "new man." The old man is under the control of his sinful nature; the new man is under the control of the Holy Spirit. Think of it as BC, before Christ, and AC, after Christ. Before Christ, you worship yourself; after Christ, you worship God. Once you are saved by grace through faith, you begin living "in" Christ – and He begins changing everything! Paul expressed it this way: *"This means that anyone who belongs to Christ has become a new person. The old life is gone; a new life has begun!"* (2 Corinthians 5:17, NLT).

When at age 16 I accepted Jesus as my Savior, I felt good about my decision to start "living for Jesus." But as months turned into years the joy I had experienced initially had waned. Something was missing. Then two men became my mentors: Oswald Chambers (through his book, *My Utmost for His Highest*), and E. Stanley Jones (through his books and personal conversations). They helped me understand the shallowness of my surrender to the Holy Spirit. I would have remained in my empty hollowness **"but the Lord"** sent those two men to show me how to let God change me!

In the words of Chambers, I had not yet signed "the death certificate" of my sinful nature. Chambers brought me to my knees as he clarified the deeper meaning of being "crucified with Christ." The following words by Chambers penetrated my heart, revealing what was missing in my life as a disciple of Jesus:

"The inescapable spiritual need each of us has is the need to sign the death certificate of our sin nature. I must take my emotional opinions and intellectual beliefs and be willing to turn them into a moral verdict against the nature of sin; that is, against any claim I have to my right to myself. Paul said, "I have been crucified with Christ...." (Galatians 2:20). He did not say, "I have made a determination to imitate Jesus Christ," or, "I will make an effort to follow Him" --- but --- "I have been **identified** with him in his death." Once I reach this moral decision and act on it, all that Christ accomplished **for** me on the Cross is accomplished **in** me. My unrestrained commitment of myself to God gives the Holy Spirit the opportunity to grant to me the holiness of Jesus Christ.

". . . it is no longer I who live. . . ." My individuality remains, but my primary motivation for living and the nature that rules me are radically changed. I have the same human body, but the old satanic right to myself has been destroyed.

". . . and the life which I now live in the flesh," not the life which I long to live or even pray that I live, but the life I now live in my mortal flesh --- the life which others can see, "I live by faith in the Son of God..." This was not Paul's own faith in Jesus Christ, but the faith in the Son God had given to him (see Ephesians 2:8). It is no longer a faith in faith, but a faith that transcends all imaginable limits --- a faith that comes only from the Son of God."

The impact of those words on me was like a lightning strike. I knew the Lord was saying to me, "You have never made an 'an absolute and irrevocable surrender' of your will to me." I knew I would never receive the faith that comes only from the Son until I made that surrender. I dropped to my knees and earnestly prayed this prayer: "Lord Jesus, I surrender my will to you absolutely and irrevocably. Please give me the grace to stay totally surrendered to you. Amen." I heard no bells or whistles but after that holy moment I began to experience the guidance and presence of the Holy Spirit in ways I had never dreamed possible. My surrender had opened the door to the life-changing power of God in all things Walter! "But the Lord"!

E. Stanley Jones helped me understand that only when I truly surrender to Jesus can I expect to receive the spiritual power to serve Jesus. Before Christ, I am dependent upon myself and my limited resources. After Christ, I am dependent upon him and the abundant resources he provides. Spiritual power is the result of a personal relationship with Jesus and the surrender of the will to him.

Jones contended that most Christians have no spiritual power because they are not abandoned to God and his purposes.[3] The pure in heart, Jones insisted, "see" the unseen; they see God because they are single-minded. Most Christians do not see God, Jones said, because they are not single-minded in heart. It's not that we don't love God but that "we do not love him completely."

I like the way Jones used the metaphor of a river and a swamp to explain his assertion that most of us give **to** God, "but we do not give **up** to him":

"The difference between a river and a swamp is that one has banks and the other has none. The swamp is very gracious and kindly, it spreads over everything, hence it is a swamp. Some of us are moral and spiritual swamps. We are so broad and liberal that we take in everything from the shady to the sacred. Hence, we are swamps. A river has banks – it confines itself to its central purpose. The civilizations of the world organize themselves not around swamps, but around rivers. There are those who refuse to tolerate anything that cuts across their central Christian purpose. They decide that there must be 'the utmost for the highest,' they cease from the divided will, become the pure in heart, the single-minded, and hence see God – see him work in and through them. Around such lives the lives of groups, of cities, of nations that begin to organize themselves. They become centers of power."

Jones then reminds us that when we tolerate everything in our lives, we must "finally tolerate our own spiritual paralysis.

---

[3] *The Christ of Every Road,* published in 1930 and republished in 2025 by the E. Stanley Jones Foundation.

Paul said, 'This one thing I do;' we would have said, 'These forty things I dabble in.' Paul was a river. We are swamps. There lies the difference."

The way to live like a river, Jones says, is to realize that all of God's resources "are back of the surrendered will." God is ready to release the power of the Holy Spirit to those whose primary goal is nothing more and nothing less than to do the will of God.

Once you are yielded to the control of the Holy Spirit, he begins producing the fruit of the Spirit in you: love, joy, peace, patience, kindness, goodness, faithfulness, gentleness and self-control. And here's the good news: You will be pleased with your new life and God will be pleased with the way you are living!

If you are reading this, you are still alive. Ask why God keeps you alive. Is it to live for yourself or to live for Him? Oswald Chambers asks if God has kept you alive "simply to be saved and sanctified." No, Chambers says, God has kept you alive so that you can "be at work in service to Him. Am I willing to be broken bread and poured out wine for Him? Am I willing to be of no value to this age or this life except for one purpose and one alone – to be used to disciple men and women to the Lord Jesus Christ. My life of service to God is the way I say 'thank you' to Him for His inexpressibly wonderful salvation" (*My Utmost for His Highest*, February 15).

When you are willing to be "broken bread and poured out wine" for Jesus, you will look for ways to serve others. And you will find so much joy in serving others that you will wish you could do more! Do you remember the film, "Schindler's List"? Knowing that Jews were being put to death, Schindler hired Jews to work in his factory. He saved about 1,200 of them. After the war ended, Schindler was broke, but began crying, "I could have done more. I could have sold my car and bought ten more. Why didn't I do more?" That was not the cry of a man who was absorbed in serving himself! It was the lament of a man who was a river, not a swamp.

Oswald Chambers invites us to realize that "all the time God is at work in our everyday events and in the people around us. If we will only obey, and do the task closest to us, we will **see** Him (boldface mine). One of the most amazing revelations of God comes to us when we learn that it is in the everyday things of life that we realize the magnificent deity of Jesus Christ" (*My Utmost for His Highest*, February 7).

William Wilberforce was an Englishman who chose to obey God by opposing the slave trade of his time. Despite the fierce opposition of those who were profiting from this ungodly business, Wilberforce almost singlehanded abolished slavery in the British Empire. Dwarfed by disease, Wilberforce was "tiny, elfish and misshapen." But one man hearing him speak said, "I saw a shrimp stand up to speak, but as I listened, he grew and grew until the shrimp became a whale." Christ does not change most of us in such a dramatic way, but he does change each of us so that we can serve him despite our handicaps and the opposition of others.

John Geddie was a Canadian missionary to the New Hebrides. There in 1848 he found a wild tribe of cannibals who loved to eat human flesh. Geddie served there 24 years. After his death, they put up a plaque in his island church that read, "In memory of John Geddie...When he landed in 1848, there were no Christians here, and when he left in 1872, there were no heathen." If I were to make a list of single-minded disciples of Jesus, Geddie's name would be at the top of the list. He was a changed man whom God used to change an entire tribe of cannibals. John Geddie was not a swamp; he was a river, a man totally surrendered to God's will for his life.

As I was completing this chapter, asking the Lord to guide me, my friend Jan Sandberg called to pray with me. She "interrupts" me once a week to spend time in intercessory prayer for friends whose needs are known to us. It is a delightful interruption, one that I welcome with joy because for several minutes Jan and I share holy communion by phone with the living Christ. Aware that I was writing this book, Jan prayed that the Lord would anoint my mind and my heart and help me complete my book and make it a blessing to many readers. I trembled with joy as Jan asked the Lord to anoint me. The Lord knew I needed Jan's prayer and he guided her to offer it. Oh the kindness of our Lord! "But the Lord"!

So, dear reader, I conclude these pages with a simple request. Stay surrendered to Jesus. Praise Him for the way his transforming grace, his divine interruptions, continue to change you into His likeness. Keep your spiritual ears open to the Holy Spirit's guidance. Be ready always to obey Him in all things great and small. Even now He may be asking you to interrupt someone's life with an expression of kindness, love and encouragement. Remember the words of Mother Teresa: "We cannot all do great things, but we can all do small things with great love."

Find ways every day to do small things with great love, and without being conscious of it, you will be living to please God. Continue living in Christ whose indwelling Spirit provides the power and grace to please God. As you pray for the Lord's guidance, imagine the joy of hearing your loving Father say to you what He once said to Moses:

And the Lord said to Moses, "I will do the very thing you have asked, because I am pleased with you and I know you by name" (Exodus 3:17).

Loving Father, as I recall my journey in faith, I thank you for every "But the Lord" interruption when your transforming grace met my need. Please continue shaping me into the likeness of my Lord Jesus, for it is my heart's desire to please you in all things. In His precious name. Amen.

Made in the USA
Columbia, SC
19 January 2026

77646876R00065